Scriptwriting Structure

TO-THE-POINT POINTERS

Bob May

Skye Bridge Publishing
Asheville, NC

Edited by D. A. Sarac
theeditingpen.com

Cover Design by Gustav Carlson
touristunknown.com

Skye Bridge Publishing
Asheville, NC
Please contact
Publisher@SkyeBridgePublishing.com

Printed in the United States of America

Scriptwriting Structure: To-the-Point Pointers / Bob May —1st ed.
ISBN 978-0-9967583-4-5

"I've spent a large portion of my life directing new plays for professional theatre and many years as well as a drama and film critic for Post-Newsweek Television. Within my experience, Bob May is about the best writer-director-teacher I know."
Davey Marlin-Jones

"I also like his directing because he teaches as he directs. I realize that community theatre is different, but nonetheless none of the other directors I've worked with have come close to being as helpful. In fact, with the theatre I've done, I've heard Bob's voice in my head more than the director's: 'Have a reason for moving; don't just move because the director told you to... Subtext! What is your subtext?... Build! Take it up a notch each time...' To the extent that I've been successful in my rules, I give credit to Bob." Juliana Flinn, Ph.D.

"Bob's focused work at UNLV has been as a playwright. He has become a highly skillful writer - his plays are adroitly plotted and very actable. He uses humor and imagination as special tools." Jerry L. Crawford

ACKNOWLEDGMENTS

Scriptwriting can be a lonely process. It is the only job in the collaborative arts of theatre and film that is done alone. Yes, scriptwriters can collaborate, but then that team is working alone. It is not until the script is written that the true collaboration begins. I have written scripts alone and with others, and there are many people I'd like to thank who have helped me throughout the years that I've been writing. First, I must thank all the students I've driven the importance of structure into since I began teaching in higher education in 1983. Critiquing the thousands of scripts I have read during that time has helped me become a better writer and teacher.

Thanks to all the producers, directors, and actors that have brought my scripts to life. They've taught me tons about writing. A big thanks to those I've written scripts with, Bryan Alan, Roy C. Booth, Chad Bradford, Violet Gunter, Mark Stephen Jensen, Karen Owings, and Cris Tibbetts. And special thanks must go to Kari Anderson, Steve Antenucci, Sharron Dilley, Bob Dryden, Dottie (May) Gunstra, Jacqueline (Mudge) Henning, Moire Lynch, Lauren May, Joe Meils, Michael Nickerson, Annie Sarac, Paula (Heckman) Schroeder, Sharon Selberg, Mark Evan Schwartz, Ralph Tropf, Llewellyn Webster, Nikki Webster, and Vicki (May) York.

And most importantly, I owe much gratitude to my mentors at UNLV, Jerry L. Crawford, Jeffery Koep, and Davey Marlin-Jones. I thought I knew how to write plays before I met them, but they opened my eyes to a wealth of knowledge that made me look at scriptwriting with a totally new mindset.

Lots of love to my wife, Cathy,
for putting up with me holed up in my office
every night as I write.

CONTENTS

FOREWORD

In the past twenty years, we have seen a huge increase in the number of playwriting degrees and courses at colleges and universities. In the past dozen years, this has evolved to include screenwriting (for television and film) and even such users as video gamers who are constantly searching for new plots. The new label at several institutions has become "Writing for Dramatic Media." It makes sense! The number of new plays produced is small in relation to the number written. One wonders how many excellent play scripts just do not "make it."

In truth, the number of plays produced professionally is small compared to the number of media scripts produced for that industry. It seems natural that gifted, trained writers would seek to use their skills to influence through the huge media marketplace.

There are a plethora of books dealing with how to sell, pitch, and market your script. *Scriptwriting Structure: To-the-Point Pointers* delves in to writing. Remember, prior to selling anything, you must have a worthy product!

It could be asked why more programs in higher education do not produce new work. The truth is that there is a great amount of new work produced, but it still does not match the total production of traditional, proven plays. We in the academy must educate our students and expose them to contemporary, modern, and classical writers. Thus, in a four-play season, we would be unlikely to see more than one original play. What are writers to do?

The answer is: "A market has been found—television, film, etc." The new question is: Do the same skills a playwright uses translate to media? Bob May has created an excellent book that relies on the basics of good writing, whether a play or film/television script. He does not attempt to instruct us on how to be an instant success but rather focuses on the basics and the use and translation of these proven fundamentals to other media.

He covers Aristotle's Six Key Elements. He includes subtext, play structure, character development, and character objectives. In short, he reminds us all of the very basis for creation of a story and how to translate the story to greatest effect in media. He, to be blunt, forces us to examine our scripts for content!

I have known Bob as a student, friend, and colleague for many years. I like to think I convinced him, having seen his excellent work as a director, that he did not need an advanced degree in directing but needed to develop his other talent and passion—writing—for him. He has continued to both write and direct with success. He is a person of the theatre who has made the transition smoothly to television and film while remaining faithful to his roots.

Bob is also an approachable, candid, and humorous person. The book captures these qualities and is the stronger for his common-sense, straightforward approach to writing. It can be of tremendous use for practicing playwrights wishing to write for media as well as aspiring playwrights who wish to learn as they develop their talents.

Jeff Koep, PhD
Professor of Theatre
Dean, College of Fine Arts 1994-2015
University of Nevada, Las Vegas

INTRODUCTION

I have spent over fifty years in the theatre, starting out as an actor, graduating to a director with over four hundred fifty productions under my belt, and finally finding a comfortable home as a playwright.

I received an MFA from the University of Nevada, Las Vegas Playwriting Program. Fifty of my plays have been produced; twenty-one of them published with hundreds of productions in the US and around the world. Of all the plays I've directed, thirty-seven of them have been originals. I've been writing plays for over forty years and teaching playwriting for half those years. I currently teach playwriting and screenwriting in the BA and MFA Creative Writing programs at the University of Central Arkansas.

When thinking about writing this book, I wasn't sure if I would write it on playwriting or screenwriting. Or maybe television writing. I decided to write it as a scriptwriting book. While the writing principles for each of the mediums are similar; the formatting is different for each one to illustrate each medium's strengths.

Scriptwriting formulas tell us plays are comprised of 75 percent dialogue and 25 percent action. Films, by contrast, are 75 percent action and 25 percent dialogue. Television is fifty-fifty. The strength of each of the mediums is exemplified by the percentages and reflected in each one's formatting. More on formatting in Chapters Seven and Eight.

Before I begin, let me use playwriting to illustrate an important point. Plays are man-made. They are not real life. Real life doesn't happen or unfold as neatly structured as a play. Just look at the spelling of the word playwright. It's wright, not write. That's right, it is wright, not write.

And why is that?

Because all plays are crafted. Just as a shipwright makes a ship or a wheelwright makes a wheel, a playwright makes a play. There are rules to follow if the playwright is going to have a structurally sound play. As a writer of scripts, you must first understand these rules so you can dissect any script.

The Pointers included throughout the book give you the tools to understand what makes a script tick. I cover many things related to scriptwriting and will discuss each one of them individually. But they don't stand alone. Many of them work with and off of each other, and in the end, they all fit together to make the whole.

-Bob May

CHAPTER 1

Dramatic Action

Dramaturgy is the study of structure. There was a time in playwriting history when there was no dramaturgical shaping. It was around 1880 right after Realism was born and during the extreme part of the Naturalism movement. In those plays, writers would take a slice of life and present it. Characters did not have objectives. They just talked or did actions without any purpose. It was often boring, because characters were doing action, but not dramatic action. Nothing was at stake. You must have something at stake and your characters must have objectives so that an audience will have some catharsis with your characters. If you know their objectives, what they are seeking, an audience can root for them to get it or to not get it.

Drama means doing or acting, so the core of all scripts is conflict/action.

The first thing to learn is the difference between action and dramatic action. Action is activity. Dramatic action is action with a purpose. All characters have a purpose (an objective). All characters try desperately to fulfill that purpose through the actions they take. They might be sidetracked by another character's purpose, but they always try to fulfill their own purpose first.

A character doesn't talk about swimming the moat to enter the castle. He jumps in and swims because he is driven by objectives and must fulfill his objective as if it were a desperate quest, as though it were a life or death situation.

Characters in plays are made up, not real people; they don't procrastinate as people do in real life. They find themselves in a situation and then fight to get out, or relieve themselves of the pressure.

If a character doesn't have purpose in what he is doing, I guarantee you the writing is not very good scriptwriting. It's usually just the writer spouting his beliefs. Oliver Stone's *JFK* is full of his theories about the JFK assassination. Many of the characters aren't speaking because they have an objective to fulfill. They are speaking to fulfill the playwright's agenda.

I read a script about Filipino mail-order brides. The playwright felt strongly about rich American men buying these women to come to America for sex, but not once in the script did I get to see how bad these men were. Characters told me how bad these men were. They were not speaking to fulfill objectives; they were spouting the playwright's beliefs from soapboxes on the subject.

Commercials and Dramatic Action

Watching television commercials is a good way to understand dramatic action. Many commercials sell the product by touting its benefits without showing dramatic action. The reasons you would want to buy the product are merely presented as a list.

The best commercials use dramatic action to sell their product. The characters in the commercials have objectives and we learn about the product as the characters try to fulfill objectives. One of my favorites was either a car or tire commercial; I think it was for tires.

There was a teenaged boy and girl talking on the phone.

The girl says, "They are leaving right now."

The boy says, "I'll be right over."

We then see the girl's parents leaving the house in the pouring rain, getting in a car, and driving off.

The boy jumps in his car and races through the rain on the way to the girl's house. When he gets to the house, he knocks on the front door.

The parents answer the door.

Moral of the commercial: Had the parents had the same kind of tires that the young boy had, they wouldn't have had to turn around and come home because of the rainstorm. Not once in the commercial does anyone say that the young man's tires were better than the parents' tires. There might have been a voice-over at the end of the commercial that identified the brand of the young man's tires.

Exercise: Dramatic Action

List your five favorite TV commercials. Do they have dramatic action to illustrate their selling points? What are your five least favorite TV commercials? Do they have dramatic action? What makes each commercial a favorite or not a favorite? I guarantee your favorites will have dramatic action and your least favorites will have action without purpose.

Identify action scene

Commercial One

Identify dramatic action (purpose)

Identify action scene

Commercial Two

Identify dramatic action (purpose)

Identify action scene

Commercial Three

Identify dramatic action (purpose)

Identify action scene

Commercial Four

Identify dramatic action (purpose)

Identify action scene

Commercial Five

Identify dramatic action (purpose)

CHAPTER 2

Objectives

I am going to spend a lot of time on objectives because objectives tie into most things I'll be discussing. Objectives are called many different things by people in the theatre: purpose, intention, motivation, goal, reason for doing something, or "the why." I prefer the term "objectives." Objectives are the characters' reasons for talking, taking action, doing anything. Objectives drive characters. As I said, characters speaking without objectives are usually just mouthpieces for the playwright's themes.

When thinking of character objectives, keep in mind that characters are always in a state of "I do," not of "I did." Always use strong active verbs to define objectives.

Examples of weak verb objectives: to get angry, to tell, to be sorry.

Examples of strong verb objectives: to belittle, to gloat, to comfort.

Every major character in your play must have a strong objective, or they are not worth writing. If you continue to write them without a strong objective, they are probably only spokes-characters supporting your theme.

Fulfilling dramatic action is the purpose for having objectives. There are two types of objectives: 1. Super objective; and 2. Unit objective.

Before I get to the two types of objectives, I should mention how objectives are discovered. In my book, *Postcard Pointers to the Performer* (Dominion Publications), I state that the given circumstances and the five Ws dictate objectives. Remember them from high school English composition class? Who? What? When? Where? Why?

You can't begin to write a character until you have answers to those five questions.

The Five Ws

Who a person is reflects heavily on how he is going to react to the other four Ws. Pee Wee Herman does things in life a whole lot differently than Arnold Schwarzenegger does. But never forget—acting is pretending. I might be Pee Wee thinking I'm Arnold.

The situation that a character is in can change how the Who does things. So the What becomes very important. What actions should the character take? The best way to find what the actions are is to ask the "magic if" question: What would I do if I were that person in those circumstances?

A five-year-old reacts (does a What) differently than a fifty-year-old when each sees a Power Ranger. Just think of what Tom Hanks did in *Big*.

When is the action happening? I know I react a heck of a lot slower in the morning than I do at night, but I'm a night person. Aren't most theatre people? Until they get into film. Then they discover the early mornings of the movie world.

Keep in mind the year, too, as you answer the question of When. We Americans were acting much more innocently in the fifties than we are now in the new millennium.

Where is it happening can play an important part in what you do and how/why you do things. If you were mad at your spouse for some stupid reason, the conversation you have with her would be very different in the living room of your in-laws' house than it would be in the privacy of your own bedroom.

Why (the objective) is the most important of the five Ws. I cannot stress enough how important the Why is! If you do not understand why you are doing something, none of the techniques I am talking about will ever make any sense.

Why are you (the Who) doing the activity you are doing (the What) at the time (When) you are doing it in the place (Where) you are doing it.

You must have answers to those five questions, or you cannot proceed to write scripts. Here are two examples.

Scenario number one:

WHO: a twenty-five-year-old homeless male
WHAT: building a fire
WHEN: twenty below zero at eight p.m. on New Year's Eve, the present
WHERE: in a back alley, downtown, Minneapolis, Minnesota
WHY: to stay warm

Scenario number two:

WHO: former homeless twenty-five-year-old male, who just won the lottery
WHAT: building a fire
WHEN: eighty degrees at eight p.m. on New Year's Eve, the present
WHERE: on the beach, Honolulu, Hawaii
WHY: to impress the woman he just met with his fire-building capabilities so they can roast s'mores.

Two scenarios, two actions, one person, five Ws, add up to the perfect ten!

A film that wonderfully illustrates my two-scenario theory is *Sliding Doors*. Dustin Hoffman needed to play very different objectives (the Why) when he played Michael Dorsey in *Tootsie* and Raymond Babbitt in *Rainman*. He was brilliant in both roles. I guarantee you he answered the five Ws before he began to rehearse either role, which is why he was so convincing in both of them. He also knew a few other tricks of the trade to help him become those characters.

The key to successful acting and scriptwriting is knowing the answers to the Ws. Now on to the two types of objectives.

Super Objective

The super objective is the main thing that each character in a script wants to achieve. All characters have one, and they try to fulfill it. They try as though it were a desperate quest or a life-or-death situation.

Take *Lord of the Rings*. Frodo's super objective is to throw the ring into the volcano to save middle earth. Throwing the ring is the "What," and the "Why" is the most important part of the objective—to save middle earth. For illustration purposes, though, I'll be talking a lot about the "What."

Unit Objectives

Then there are unit objectives. Constantine Stanislavsky, the Father of Method Acting, introduced units of action. As a character seeks to fulfill the super objective, he goes through a series of actions, or units.

One of the easiest ways to note a unit change is to remember that the unit changes on every entrance or exit of a character. Let's say that you and I are talking about something secret. When another character enters, the unit changes because we are no longer talking about the secret thing. The new character is going to dictate a new objective. Even if the new character is in on the secret, the objective changes because we are talking about the secretive issue with new information, or we are filling the new person in on the conversation.

However, units can also change without an entrance or exit. Think of it this way: characters, as they try to fulfill their super objective, are bombarded with things that get in the way of their fulfilling the super objective. Sometimes characters fulfill unit objectives and they move on to the next unit and objective, but other times characters don't fulfill a unit objective because another character forces them into the new unit, or the new circumstances just dictate that they don't fulfill the objective. Characters should never look backward– they should always move forward, trying to fulfill their next unit objective as they seek to fulfill their super objective.

Those things (units) are up to you as the writer. In other words, if I'm walking to the door or I'm Frodo walking to the volcano, and nothing gets in my way, that's boring. If you write a play or film like that, there is no conflict. And the core of all drama, of all scripts, is conflict.

However, if I'm walking across a room because I want to get to the door, and let's say a chair falls in front of me, I have to deal with it. Once I deal with the chair, I keep going to where? To the door, my super objective. I must fulfill my super objective. Then a person gets in my way, another unit. This person has a super objective, too, that he is trying to fulfill. That creates conflict, which is the core of all scripts and makes the script interesting.

Beats

Units can be broken into beats. Beats are all the different ways a character goes about trying to fulfill the unit objectives. To illustrate, I'll ask someone for five bucks. That person is just going to keep saying no.

> BOB

Can I have $5?

> PERSON

No.

> BOB

Can I PLEASE have five dollars?

> PERSON

No.

> BOB

If I don't get the five bucks, bad things are going to happen to me.

> PERSON

No.

> BOB

Remember the last time you needed five dollars ... I gave you five dollars?

> PERSON

No.

> BOB
> If you don't give me five bucks, I'll break your kneecaps!

> PERSON
>
> No.

> BOB
>
> The heck with you.

I then leave, ending that unit.

There are five beats within that unit. I tried to go about getting what I wanted in five different ways. I asked politely, I begged, I tried to get sympathy, I tried to use guilt, and then I threatened. In a script, each beat wouldn't be just one line. The character would exhaust each avenue (beat) before moving to the next. The other character would also try to fulfill his or her objective.

Remember, sometimes characters fulfill the unit objective, and sometimes they do not. If they don't, they never look back. They always look forward to fulfill their super objective.

Super Objective Improv

Here's an improvisation I use in class to illustrate how all characters need objectives, yet most beginning writers only give one of the characters in a scene an objective. A male student goes over to a female friend's apartment and asks her for something, anything. They are good friends. Because she knows him, she can't dismiss him. Whatever he asks for, she can't give it to him, no matter what he asks for. By not giving him what he wants, I am creating conflict. Remember, conflict is the core of all drama.

The scene usually goes something like this.

> (The MALE knocks on door.)

FEMALE
Who is it?

> (MALE says his name.)

FEMALE (cont'd)
Oh, hi, come on in.

MALE
You know those books for class I loaned you two weeks ago?

FEMALE
Oh, yeah!

MALE
Do you still have them? I would really appreciate if I could get them back.

FEMALE
I don't have any idea where they are. I thought I gave
them back to you.

MALE
No, you didn't, and I really need them.

FEMALE
Well, I don't have them here.

MALE
Do you mind if I look around here then?

FEMALE
Don't you believe me?

MALE
I believe you. I'm still going to look around because I
know how you are with losing things.

What's his super objective? To get the book. What's
hers? To not give him the book? No, that is her unit
objective. You have to remember that she is not sitting
in her apartment waiting for him to come over and
ask for something. I then have the male student knock
on my door and ask me for something. The same
rules apply. Here's the same scenario with two super
objectives.

MALE
You know those books for class I loaned you two weeks
ago?

BOB

I thought I gave them back to you. Look, this is not a good time; I have to get these tests graded before rehearsal tonight.

MALE

I need those books to study tonight.

BOB

Really, this is not a good time. But you can come back and look tomorrow if you want.

MALE

How does that help me study tonight?

BOB

Go ask (says name of girl who did previous improv) to borrow her books. Right now I need you to get out of my apartment! I'm sorry you lost your book, but I have to get back to grading.

Now what's my super objective? Yes, to get the tests graded. In the first scene, the female fell into what the male wanted and didn't have her own objective. There was nothing stopping my character from trying to help the guy get some books. I just couldn't give them to him. That's why I suggested he go ask the girl. I was doing that so I could fulfill my super objective of grading the tests.

Homeland

Homeland is a wonderful series on Showtime. Claire Danes' character has a problem where she has to take medication. If she doesn't take it, she kind of goes crazy. She needs to get some meds because she doesn't have any. Her father has the same ailment, but she can't tell her father that she hasn't been taking her meds. So she goes over to his house to steal some of his meds. She isn't going to tell him this.

An example of bad writing would be if she comes into the house and says,

"Hi, Dad, how are you?"

"I'm doing great, how are you?"

"I'm doing great, really well."

Follow me? The father has no life of his own.

Now let's look at better writing. She enters the house and says,

"Hi, Daddy."

He's ironing clothes and says, "Oh, well, hi, honey. Can I get you a sandwich?"

You know how parents are; they always want to give their children food. See what they did? They gave him a life, he was doing something. He's not there just to answer her questions.

She then replies, "Oh, no, I'm fine. Thank you. Can I use your restroom?"

We all know what she's there for and why she's going up to the bathroom. She's going to steal his meds. But he doesn't know that. It was such a nice little scene. The father was doing things. He wasn't just sitting around waiting for her to come over, because he didn't know she was coming over.

As scriptwriters, you have to give all your characters objectives. I can't tell you how many times I read a scene and only one character has an objective. I call that playing Ed McMahon to Johnny Carson on *The Tonight Show*. Ed just agreed with everything Johnny said. He didn't have his own life, his own objective. That is how it is in many scripts I read: one character is just there to support another character. That makes for bad scripts and bad character development.

A Taxi Driver and Me

In my book, *Postcard Pointers to the Performer*, I explain objectives in another way.

All characters, in any play, must have a super objective. That objective gives them their life. It dominates everything they do.

I live in Little Rock, Arkansas, and I've just finished writing my latest play. Let's say that I have to get the manuscript to my agent in New York City at 45th and Broadway by noon on Wednesday. If I get it there on time, I get a ten thousand dollar bonus. By doing that, I upped the stakes on my objective.

I leave my home on Tuesday in plenty of time to get to NYC by the deadline. However, because it's winter, I have problems. Snow and ice prevent me from fulfilling my perfect travel plans. I finally get there, but with only minutes to spare.

I race out of the terminal and jump into the cab at the front of the long line of taxis and say to the driver,

"If you can get me to 45th and Broadway by eleven o'clock, I'll give you a $500 tip."

The taxi driver answers, "Sure, buddy, I'll get you there in no time flat."

That's bad writing. Why? Yes, the driver doesn't have a life or an objective.

Let's give him a life. He is a thirty-year-old male who thinks his wife is having an affair with the Jewish gentleman who owns the delicatessen next to the Manhattan flat where he and his wife live.

So now I jump into the taxi with the same objective. I must get my play to my agent by eleven. I say, "Get me to 45th and Broadway by noon and I'll give you $500 tip!"

Now we have a mad, jealous husband, taxi cab driver (with a life), who is not having a good day. He has a gun sitting on the front seat. He responds, "Get out of my cab. I don't feel like helping anyone today."

I plead with him.

The taxi driver points the gun at me and tells me to get out of the cab.

I explain my dilemma to the driver.

The driver tells his problems. "My wife is cheating, and I'm going to kill the deli owner she's sleeping with."

I continue to argue with the cab driver and finally say, "Look, if you get me there by eleven, I'll help you kill the deli owner!"

Both of those characters had their own lives. They had their own objectives to fulfill. Their paths happened to cross, creating conflict. They eventually fulfilled their main objectives by helping one another.

Their objectives were filled, but the path had lots of speed bumps.

It should be clear that those examples of super objectives are personal to the character. Characters are selfish; they want something for themselves. That is not to say that they don't want things for other people, like a mother wanting to protect her children, but always make the super objective a personal want of the character.

Characters need super objectives to create conflict. Otherwise, a complication doesn't matter—they would just deal with it and move on.

Units and Objectives – The Backyard Story

I've explained that unit objectives are all the objectives characters try to fulfill as they seek their super objective. Here's my famous backyard story to illustrate objectives and unit changes. In 1993, I had a big, magical backyard at my house in Minnesota. Coming out the back door, there was a stoop with three steps leading down to a sidewalk. At the right side of the yard, the sidewalk led to a fence with a gate at the back of the yard and then an alley. In the alley to the left of the gate were my garbage cans.

I'll illustrate unit objectives with the "What," even though I told you objectives are really about the "What" and the "Why."

I have a date tonight. My super objective "Why" is I want to impress my future wife, Cathy, with a clean house. My super objective "What" is to get the garbage from the house to the garbage cans in the alley. It is the same thing as Frodo going from place to place in fulfillment of throwing the ring into the volcano.

After bagging up the garbage in the kitchen, I head toward the back door. I find it locked with a dead bolt that needs a key for both sides. So I set the garbage down by the door and go back to get the key. Now the unit is changing and so is the objective—to get the key. The key is in the utility drawer in the kitchen. I get the key and then walk back to the door, unlock it, fulfilling that objective, and moving back to the super objective, to get the garbage to the cans in the alley.

Remember, a character always tries to get back to fulfilling the super objective.

I pick up the garbage bag and push on the door. But the door won't open because there's snow on the back stoop.

As a scriptwriter, I can have the character decide on options, just like in real life. I can take the garbage out the front door because I have already shoveled the front steps; or, leave the garbage bag by the back door since I need to shovel the back stoop anyway.

So the unit changes again as I walk out the front door, grab the shovel, walk around to the back of the house, and shovel the back stoop off. Now everything is once again in order for me to get back to my super objective. I open the door, grab the garbage, and start down the sidewalk.

I have divided my backyard into three sections.

Remember it was 1993. I recall that because *Jurassic Park* had just come out when I first began telling this story. Picture in your head the velociraptors, those crazy little dinosaurs at the end of the film that were really mean.

The first section of my yard is full of velociraptors, and they begin to attack me. The unit changes, and now my objective is to save myself. I begin to use the loaded garbage bag as a weapon. It's a Glad Forceflex bag, so it's tough. I kill and maim the little demons as I fight my way down the sidewalk. If I had stopped and talked to one, that would be a beat in this unit, but there's no talking to velociraptors. I manage to get through this unit/that part of my yard and cross into the middle of the three sections in the backyard.

This section of the yard is where the fraternities on campus have their parties. This one fraternity is having a big kegger. One of my students sees me walking down the sidewalk and says, "Hey, come have a beer." After the fight I just went through, I could use a breather and something to drink, so I put the garbage bag down on the sidewalk and enter a different world. And as I do so, the unit and objective changes.

As I am enjoying a beer, another student comes up to me and says, "Hey, why did you give me a D?" That changes the unit again. Other students are coming up and asking me questions about reading their scripts and so on. Finally remembering the waiting garbage bag, I say, "I have to go."

The unit changes. I get up and go back to my super objective.

As I continue down the sidewalk, I enter the third section of my backyard. A few of the students ask me if I'd like to catch some rays. Yes, I know, it was snowing back at my back door, and now people are sunbathing. I said my backyard was magical.

It always amazed me that after a cold winter the temperature could be fifty degrees and people would be hanging out on their dorm balconies or on towels on the campus grounds wearing their bathing suits, soaking up the sun! I grew up in Florida, so fifty degrees is cold!

I said, "No, I can't do that."

But they drag me into their unit, and I have a pleasant conversation about the new president sworn in on January 20 of that year, William J. Clinton.

When some Young Republicans (which is rare in Minnesota) start in on what a great president George H. W. Bush Sr. was, I take my leave.

Back to the sidewalk, the garbage, and my super objective.

I finally get to the back gate, and what do I find? It is locked, and the key is in the utility drawer back in the kitchen. I leave the garbage bag by the back gate and head back to the house, changing units as I go. I sunbathe. I drink some more beer. I fight off more velociraptors, this time with my bare hands.

I get the key and grab a machete. (This bit was added after seeing Robert Rodriguez's *Machete*). I use it to fight my way through the velociraptors once again and proudly display the blood-soaked weapon as I have a few more beers with the fraternity. Then I use it to frighten off the sunbathing, Bush-praising Republicans.

Finally arriving at my gate, I raise the machete high above my head in what I think is a climactic gesture as I unlock the gate, walk through it, and ...

I look for my garbage cans, but someone stole them!

So what do I do in the end? I throw my garbage in the neighbor's garbage cans and fulfill my super objective. I celebrate my victory and wrap up the loose ends by bypassing the sunning Republicans, having a few more beers with the frat boys, stepping through all the dead velociraptors, and getting home in time to let Cathy in the front door.

But you see what I'm doing? Every time I try to fulfill my super objective, something got in my way. As scriptwriters, those things are up to you. You come up with these obstacles. They don't have to be physical obstacles. Sometimes the best obstacles are psychological obstacles. A combination of both psychological obstacles and physical obstacles are actually best. What's Frodo's psychological obstacle? The ring's power. That's a big obstacle. All good scripts deal with both kinds.

Discovering Units and Beats

The following is a true story that happened to me one morning. I wrote down the events because it was so theatrical as the stakes kept rising. I now give it to my classes and ask them to break it into units and beats. I have them put a red slash in the story where the unit changes and a green slash where there is a beat change. They have to come up with a super objective for the characters and objectives for each unit. I wrote it as one paragraph because breaking it into paragraphs would help indicate where units and beats begin and end.

My wife, Cathy, has to be to work at seven in the morning, two hours before I do. She gets up at 4:45 and leaves the house by 6:15. I usually can sleep for another hour, but this morning I have to get up when she leaves because I have an important meeting at the university at eight a.m. that I can't miss. So the day begins:

We are both sleeping soundly in our queen-sized bed with our three miniature schnauzers between us. The alarm goes off at the regularly scheduled time, which jolts both of us awake. Cathy reaches over and hits snooze, and we both go back to sleep. Nine minutes later, the alarm sounds again. This time Cathy turns it off and gets out of bed. I turn over and go back to sleep, luckily not hearing her as she gets ready for work. The next thing I know, she is waking me up to kiss me and say good-bye. I reply with an "I love you" and roll over, wanting to go back to sleep again. She reminds me of my meeting, not that I need reminding. She leaves, and I get out of bed and walk into the bathroom. Not even five minutes later Cathy comes back into the house and says, "A tree fell on the fence by the front gate, and the fence is low enough that Maggie can get out." Maggie is our Great Pyrenees who loves to roam. I wash the shaving cream off my face, get dressed, and Cathy and I go outside. We say our good-byes again; she gets in her car and drives away. I assess the damage and decide the first thing I need to do is get Maggie in the house. I finally manage to do that. I walk to the front gate and try to lift the tree off the fence, but it is too heavy, so I walk to the barn and grab the chain saw. The front gate and the barn are the length of two football fields apart, so the walk from the gate to the barn is a bit of a trek. Back at the gate, I start the chain saw and begin to cut the tree on the side that is hanging over the fence. The circumference of the tree is about the size of a Frisbee. About halfway through the tree, the chain saw runs out of gas, and the gas can is back in the barn. I walk back to the barn, and on my way it begins to rain–heavily. I almost decide to stop the task and just keep the dog in the house all day long so she cannot get out and run, but I don't. I march on to get the gas can. When I grab the can, I am angry to learn that it is empty, so I grab the hand saw and head back through the rain to the gate. A neighbor friend of mine who needs some jumper cables to start his car greets me at the gate. I explain to him I don't have time to jump his car but tell him where he can find the jumper cables in the barn. As he walks to the barn, I begin to saw through the rest of the tree with the handsaw. I then try to lift the tree off the fence, but it is still too heavy. About that time, my neighbor has walked back to gate. I ask him to help me lift the tree off the fence. We both manage to toss the tree to one side of the fence. I'll deal with cutting it up and moving it when I return home that afternoon. The neighbor says, "Thanks for the cables," and leaves. I jury-rig the fence the best that I can, enough that Maggie can't get out. I grab all the tools and head to the barn. Inside, I feed the donkeys. I usually do that when I first get up. As I walk back to the house, the rain stops. On the front porch, I strip out of my soaking wet clothes, then head in to take a shower, but when I stare at the clock, I see that I don't have time. I figure the rain was like a shower. I get dressed and head out the front door. Letting Maggie out as I go. I jump in my truck and make it to the meeting with only minutes to spare.

Don't read the following paragraph until you've written down the super objectives of the characters and broken the story into units.

Most students think my super objective is to remove the tree. That becomes what the story is about, but it is a unit objective. What is my super objective? To get to the meeting on time. How did you do? Now break the story into units and beats.

The Through-Line or the Spine of the Character and Other Useful Unit Information

Another way of talking about each of the units in the "Backyard Story" is referring to all of the units collectively as the through-line or spine of the character. The through-line is all the objectives strung together from the beginning of the script until the end of the script when the character has achieved his or her super objective. The spine is also each unit as a vertebra in the character's spine/life. They mean the same thing; it's once again theatre people calling one thing by different names.

The common link between the above stories illustrating objectives, this next story, and all scripts, is they all possess a beginning, middle, and end. They introduce a problem, they develop that problem, and the problem comes to a climax. Each unit also reveals different aspects of the plot/story such as mood, character, transitions, conflict, or storytelling. Some units reveal just one of the aspects, others can reveal several of them.

Another common denominator in all scripts is that each major character starts with an attitude at the beginning of the script and, by the end of the play, the character has a different attitude. We refer to this as polar attitudes.

Look at Scrooge in *A Christmas Carol* by Charles Dickens. His super objective is to live and have a good life, even if it means being unkind to all around him. His polar attitude at the beginning of the play shows that he hoards his money, and by the end of the play, his polar attitude shows him giving his money away. The road he travels from one attitude to the other is made up of plot events or units of action, the through-line, or his spine.

The story begins with a mood unit revealing the working conditions at Scrooge's shop. Bob Cratchit forces Scrooge into a new character unit when he asks for Christmas Day off.

"Bah humbug," says Scrooge to Cratchit. Scrooge's unit objective is keep a tight reign on his business. He reluctantly gives Cratchit Christmas off but without pay.

In another character unit, Scrooge's nephew, Fred, visits the shop and invites Scrooge to his home for a Christmas Eve celebration. Scrooge takes this opportunity (objective) to spout his views on Christmas.

While Scrooge is shopping in town, a mood and character unit is set as the townspeople look down on him, but he gets the upper hand by reminding some people of the money they owe him, ignoring others, and focusing on the shopping tasks at hand.

At his home, he sees Jacob Marley in the door knocker, which forces him into a new mood (character unit), but Scrooge blames the vision on his being tired. Scrooge then eats, satisfying the transitional unit objective of eating because he is hungry, and prepares for bed.

Marley then visits Scrooge's house and warns him that he must change his lifestyle or end up in Hades adorned in heavy chains. This sets what is at stake in the script: Will Scrooge change his lifestyle? Scrooge counters this conflict and storytelling unit with denial that Marley could come back from the dead.

Marley then says, "You will be visited by three spirits tonight." Scrooge shrugs off this storytelling beat with more denial and goes to bed.

The Ghost of Christmas Past visits and takes Scrooge through several storytelling units of his past. We learn Scrooge is a lonely lad, we meet his loving sister (who died at a young age), we see Scrooge as a happy young man, working for Fezziwig, and falling in love with Fezziwig's daughter, Belle. We see his greed and lust for wealth destroy his relationship with his fiancé, Belle.

The Ghost of Christmas Past forces Scrooge into these units. His objective is to show Scrooge that he wasn't always an unhappy, unkind person. Scrooge, of course, is in denial and wants to go back to bed, but he eventually has questions. However, the Ghost is gone before Scrooge can get answers.

Using several storytelling, character, and mood units, The Ghost of Christmas Present's objective is to show Scrooge the good in his nephew and the life that Bob Cratchit lives. Scrooge realizes that if he goes along with the Present Ghost's shenanigans, the sooner it will be over.

Just as Scrooge is beginning to feel some sympathy, the unit is changed by the arrival of the Ghost of Christmas Future who shows Scrooge that he will die a hated, lonely man, and rot in Hades.

Scrooge wakes up from his dream and realizes he must be a better person.

That is a quick synopsis of the units that Scrooge faces, and there are a lot more than what I've written. He has fulfilled his super objective of having a good life, but he is going about it in a different way now because his polar attitude has changed, brought on by all the units of action in his through-line or spine. So that's super objectives and unit objectives. Do you understand the difference between the two?

Autobiographical Monologue

The following is an exercise I have been using for years to develop characters and their objectives. The former Head of Playwriting at UNLV and my mentor, Dr. Jerry L. Crawford, wrote this exercise, and it is used here with his permission. I assign it at the beginning of each semester, and as an added bonus, it helps the students get to know one another. After each student reads their monologues to the class, we discuss the character, diction, and objective.

The challenge is that your "actor/speaker/character" must answer all the questions in the Exercise in a single page. Thus, compression is mandatory. However, you may use as small a font size as you wish.

The character shouldn't just be reciting a list. Giving the character a clear objective makes this exercise work best.

Here are some examples of actual monologues written by students in my classes. I have changed the names and only included the beginnings of each monologue, but you can get the gist of each one.

In a secluded corner of a tavern, four women sit around Succumbam, a muse who is doing her best to forget her name with the ever-rising number of drinks she is consuming. She speaks, "Dionysius, guide me tonight. The Fates gave me one hell of a project. Hell, I couldn't even crack him. I had to go back in for reassignment. Unfortunately, that's why I got you girls here. I have to find my own replacement for that wimp. And I know how you girls love a challenge. Who is he? George Spelvin. The name is already making me want another drink. Little rat-faced, prima donna, writing major from that middle of nowhere shantytown called Podunk. Makes Tartarus look like Paradise, let me tell you. He went to the equally redneck town of Smallville for his high school. He couldn't get any more normal, I swear. No divine origin; Zeus didn't rape his mother or anything."

A young male character says, "Gentlemen, please have a seat. All right, so let's just get down to it, shall we? This is your mark right here: George Spelvin. A real pretentious jerk. Now, I don't care what method you use to deal with him. Shoot him, eat him, swallow his soul for all I care, just kill him and put him out of my misery. I have known that chancrous ass ever since we went to Smallville High School together."

A private detective speaks. "Hello, Bob and Cathy, correct? Yes, of course I got your call. Why else would I be here if I hadn't agreed to take the case? May I come in? Something to drink? Water or tea would be lovely. I'm not one to chat, so unpleasantries over, let's get started. From your message, though it was hard to decipher with all the sobbing, I was able to deduce your daughter, Georgina Spelvin, is missing. I knew she was your child because otherwise, why would you be bothering a consulting detective with your problems. She went missing about a week or so ago, am I correct? From her University. The University of Central Arkansas? Why would someone from Texas, especially the Dallas area, attend school in Conway? No, don't answer that."

A young woman enters a store called Party City. "Hello, I am here to speak to someone about planning a birthday party. Oh, that's you? Okay, it's for my husband, George Spelvin. The date? July 4. He will be turning twenty-three. Now, I was thinking of having a movie theme for his party. Could we do that? Okay, great. Yeah, being a film major at UCA, I think he would like that. I thought we might display some posters from movies like *Batman* or any movies by Martin Scorsese. He also is a big *Battlestar Galactica* fan, so he would enjoy that too. Music in the background would be nice. I know that he has been listening to the new Kings of Leon album recently, and he would probably like to have that playing at his party."

You will notice that we learn just as much about the speaker as we do about the person of whom they are speaking. In each case, an MDQ (Major Dramatic Question) is set too. I will be discussing MDQ later on.

Exercise: Autobiographical Monologue

Create a one-page, single-spaced, typed, autobiographical monologue for a solo actor in which a fictional character is relating things about you and your life to an assemblage of people. You must also create the situation of the assemblage. The monologue must relate the following information:

- Full name and the name you wish to be called
- Major or status in school
- Schools attended including high school
- Major in college
- Occupation, if any (part-time job?)
- Where you were born and primarily raised
- Parents' names, occupation, deceased or living – if living, where?
- Same with brothers, sisters, children, spouse, if any
- Background in writing – kinds, publications? Productions?
- Background in theatre aside from writing
- Favorite specific subject in all years of schooling
- Clarify how you write – longhand or computer
- Favorite playwright and play (living and dead)
- Favorite actor and actress (living and dead)
- Favorite director (living or dead)
- Favorite novelist (living or dead)
- Favorite poet (living or dead)
- Favorite composer (living or dead)

- Favorite singer (living or dead)
- Favorite film
- Favorite television program
- Favorite hobby
- Special interests
- Career goals and aspirations
- Name your most redeeming quality and your most limiting quality – both as a writer and as a person
- What was the saddest event of your life and what was the happiest event of your life.

CHAPTER 3

Subtext

Does everyone know what subtext is? Subtext is what is being said, not just the words the character is actually speaking. Characters usually don't tell the truth. There is usually more to what is being said. They are trying to fulfill their objectives, so they go about it by not saying what's on their minds. Actors and audiences can hear the subtext in every line spoken onstage.

Here are some subtext illustrations.

I'm Fine

I am walking across campus, see a friend, and say, "Hi, how are you?" He says, "I'm FINE!" But he doesn't say it as if he is fine. I hear the subtext, which is, "I don't want to talk right now," and know there's something wrong. Obviously, he is not fine. If I take him literally, I keep on walking. He told me he was fine.

I then say, "What's wrong?"

He replies, "Nothing."

I hear more subtext, which is, "leave me alone."

If I keep talking to him, he might eventually tell me what is bothering him.

Usually when writing scripts, you don't want to write the subtext, but you want to write so the subtext comes out. Who, what, when, where, and why also dictate the subtext.

I Love You

Consider all the different ways a person can say, "I love you." These are just three words spoken between many couples, but do they always imply what the words infer? Here is an example of what I mean.

Who: a twenty-year-old male college student

What: answering after being confronted by the female student he is dating

When: at night after a dinner date

Where: her dorm room

Why: to let her down easily

When he says, "I love you," the subtext is, "but not in the way you want me to." The same young man would say, "I love you," differently if his subtext was, "if you force me to say it, I will."

Dogs and Subtext

Dogs don't understand words; they understand subtext. Yes, some dogs know words like "sit," or "go out," but if I say in a very sweet voice, "come here, let me hit you on the top of the head," the dog comes right to me because it is hearing the sweet subtext.

Follow the Show Subtextually

I'm a big believer that you can watch a play in a language you don't speak, and if the actors are good at subtext and the play has been staged properly, you will be able to follow the plot. Most people follow the plot of opera through the subtext and the movement.

I'll say, "I love you" three different ways. I'll say it in a monotone each time so there's no subtext. However, the movement will tell you what those three words really mean. First I'll stand still, no movement, and say, "I love you." Now I'll say it as I walk toward you. "I love you." Now I'll say it as I walk away from you. "I love you."

You can pick up on the subtext with movement. No movement means I am indifferent. Walking toward you shows I really love you, and walking away as I say it means I don't really love you. The movement pattern tells you the story. Even in another language, you could follow the plot because of the subtext and movement.

As playwrights, you have to understand what subtext is. When writing, you must write subtextually. Directors and actors follow the actions of the characters subtextually. If you just go by the text, you won't get anywhere. Remember, characters are usually not telling the truth!

For the actor and director, the script is already written. But the playwright has to divide the script into units and beats, figure out what the objectives are for the units, and figure out how to say the subtext without actually saying it in the lines.

Exercise: Subtext

There are dozens of ways to say, "I love you." Establish a character by answering the five "W" questions (who, what, when, where, and why) and then say those three words using the subtext you have come up with and see if the class can guess the subtext.

The key is not to paraphrase the line. What new information is learned by the words that are being said?

Another Subtext Exercise

In many plays, the subtext must be heard to fully understand the story. It is a completely different experience to follow them subtextually than if you follow them literally. Read any play by Chekhov (*The Cherry Orchard, The Sea Gull, The Three Sisters*) or *Waiting for Godot* by Samuel Beckett, and then view a live production of the script. It will probably be easier if you watch a film version of the script. I use *Waiting for Godot* in my classes.

Can you think of any others?

CHAPTER 4

Protagonist / Antagonist

What is the definition of a protagonist? The main character? That's what most people say. And it usually is the main character. But the definition I want you to remember is this: A protagonist is the character who drives the action forward.

A lot of students will also say the protagonist is the good person. But there are some bad protagonists. Dexter is not a good person. Walter White in *Breaking Bad* isn't a good person. He started out as a good person, but his whole character went to the dark side. It didn't happen all at once. It starts from the beginning when he gets that guy in the basement, remember?

What is a Character Willing to Do?

A character's actions show what he is willing to do to achieve his super objective. It is important to know what a character is willing to do to fulfill that objective. If you don't know that, you can't write that character.

Because the *Breaking Bad* writers wrote that in the first season, does anyone care if I give the end away? He kills someone. But you see from the beginning he has big psychological issues. It tells you what his character is capable of doing. Over the six seasons, he did some horrendous things. But you still cared for him, right?

Your Antagonist Should Be as Strong as Your Protagonist

The antagonist, by definition, is the person who gets in the way of the protagonist fulfilling his or her super objective. If you make your antagonist as strong as your protagonist, you will have some great conflict.

Agnes of God

Agnes of God, by John Pielmeier, is a powerful play with a strong antagonist and protagonist. The play deals with Christianity. A young nun, Agnes, has given birth to a baby that is discovered dead in a trash can in the young nun's convent room.

Two strong characters equally deal with both sides of the Christianity issue. There is a Mother Superior supporting the Christian viewpoint. And to represent the anti-Christianity viewpoint, there is a chain smoking, ex-Catholic psychiatrist, whose sister died in a convent, and who is at the convent to investigate what happened. The two go up against each other. The antagonist and protagonist are equally strong, and it makes for a really good play. In the movie version, Jane Fonda plays the psychiatrist and Anne Bancroft is the Mother Superior.

In a two-person play, the protagonist and antagonist alternate between the characters, each becoming the other's antagonist. The end of the script reveals the stronger protagonist by which side of the issue wins out.

At the end of *Agnes*, is the play pro- or anti-Christianity? It is pro, and one would think it is because of the Mother Superior's argument. That is somewhat true, but the psychiatrist has stopped smoking, she has gone back to attending church, and she's found her religion again. So the psychiatrist is the strongest protagonist of the piece because the psychiatrist makes the biggest change in character.

Keely and Du

There's another play called *Keely and Du* by Jane Martin, about the abortion debate. Two right-to-lifers kidnap a young rape victim (Keely) as she's walking into an abortion clinic to have an abortion. They take her to a warehouse, dress her in hospital garb, handcuff her to a bed, and they hire a nurse (Du) to care for her.

They say to her, "You're not leaving this warehouse until you have this baby."

Of course she says, "You can't make me have this baby! It's my choice."

Thus both sides of the abortion issue are represented in the play.

Who's the protagonist? The young girl, Keely, is because in the end, her side wins out. If you can call what happens winning–her viewpoint wins out over the other. The writer believes this way over the other, making abortion illegal doesn't stop it.

You want both your protagonist and antagonist equally strong.

Othello

The classic example of an equally strong protagonist and antagonist is in *Othello*. Othello is the classic protagonist, but I've had many discussions where people think Iago is the protagonist because he's just as strong as Othello. At the end of the play, Othello smothers his wife for being unfaithful, and it is his character who makes the biggest change.

Yes, it was Iago who fooled Othello into taking that action against his wife, and there are good arguments about Iago driving the action over Othello, but in the end Shakespeare called the play *Othello*, not Iago.

Classic Protagonist / Antagonist List

SCRIPT	PROTAGONIST	ANTAGONIST
Sweeney Todd	Sweeney	Judge Turpin
Robin Hood	Robin	The Sheriff
Harry Potter	Harry	Voldemort
Lord of the Rings	Frodo	Sauron
Star Wars	Luke Skywalker	Darth Vader
A Streetcar Named Desire	Blanche	Stanley

A "Thing" as Antagonist

The antagonist doesn't have to be a person/character. One could say that the antagonist is the "thing" that gets in the way of the protagonist getting what he or she wants, and I don't mean John Carpenter's *Thing* (even though the Thing is not a person).

The antagonist could be an idea, the world, the environment, the setting, the elements, social influences, the work world, an institution, a disease, or even the protagonist himself.

If the antagonist isn't a person/character, it is always good to personify the "thing" at some point in the script to speak for the "thing" or a champion for the cause. *A Few Good Men* is a great example of this. The protagonist, Lt. Daniel Kaffee, is up against the military establishment, personified wonderfully by Col. Nathan R. Jessup, and played brilliantly by Jack Nicholson in the film.

When I adapted *Rudolph the Red Nosed Reindeer* for the stage, I found that the story didn't have a clear antagonist. The reindeer would not let Rudolph join in the reindeer games, but there wasn't a clear personified antagonist. Winter was preventing the reindeer from seeing clearly as the sleigh flew in the Christmas Eve night, so I personified winter as Old Man Winter, and he was having a conflict with Mother Nature, so he was making it snow very heavily the night before Christmas. With Rudolph's bright red nose, he could guide the sleigh through the blinding snowstorm.

In the TV movie adaptation of *Rudolph*, the antagonist was the Abominable Snowman.

Scripts with "Things" as Antagonists

Here is a list of classic scripts with antagonists who are not people. Try to name the antagonist in each script.

A.
Perfect Storm
Twister
Sleepless in Seattle
American Beauty
Cast Away

B.
American Pie?
Dr. Jekyll and Mr. Hyde?

(Answers A: 1. the weather, 2. the weather, 3. distance between the two, 4. society, 5. the island)
(Answer B: The protagonist is his own antagonist)

Exercise: Protagonist / Antagonist

Read several two-character plays and decide which is the protagonist and antagonist. Some suggestions are:

'night Mother by Marsha Norman
The Gin Game by Donald L. Coburn
The Tiger by Murray Schisgal
The Typists by Schisgal
The Fourposter by Jan de Hartog

Exercise: Protagonist and also Antagonist

Read several plays and list the titles of those which have a Protagonist who is also his or her own Antagonist. Here are three examples:

A Clockwork Orange
Dr. Jekyll and Mr. Hyde
Leaving Las Vegas

CHAPTER 5

Aristotle's Six Key Elements of Drama

Aristotle is known mostly for being a philosopher, but he is also known as the Father of Modern Playwriting Criticism. For an ancient Greek philosopher, he sure had many valid points that still stand up in modern scriptwriting. His teachings have stood the test of time, and many of his theories are the foundation of all playwriting pedagogy. Even Hollywood uses Aristotle as a foundation for scripts. Read *Aristotle's Poetics for Screenwriters* by Michael Tierno.

The Poetics

Aristotle's book, *The Poetics*, contains much useful fodder for any playwright's attack on the craft of writing plays. If you have not read *The Poetics*, I suggest that you read it. It's not an easy read, but the best translation/ adaptation of the book that I've read is by Gerald Else.

One of the most important theories his book contains is that all plays must include six key elements to be successful. And there is a hierarchy to the importance of the elements.

Plot
Character
Theme
Diction
Music
Spectacle

Plot

According to Aristotle, plot is the most important element. That is very logical. All scripts must have a plot. A definition of plot could be story. But let's go a little further. It's *What* about the story? Action. Elements. Things that happen to make up the story. In *The Lord of the Rings* trilogy, all the struggles that Frodo faces as he makes his quest to throw the ring in the volcano are plot.

These events are the units that happen that make up the story or the plot. Remember I said all these things tie together? So, plot consists of the unit objectives strung together; they can also be called units of action.

Plot is number one. You need to have a plot. If you have a strong plot, you will probably have strong characters.

Character

Number two is character or characters. A definition of characters could be the individuals in the story. The individuals who do what? They carry out all the actions/events that make up plot; all the actions that we just talked about. And make sure all your characters have different personalities.

A problem with many writers—and I'm included in this too—is when they start writing characters, they use themselves for all the characters, because they are most familiar with themselves. That's why good writers should keep journals, because if you see something interesting that someone does, you can write it down. It gives you material to use outside yourself.

As a writer, you should be keeping a journal. Not a diary but a journal. In it, write down things you observe about people through the day—the way they dress, walk, handle the objects they use, and the way they eat.

There was a woman I used to work with who did the craziest thing when eating. At the end of every meal, she left a bit of food on her plate. She might even go back for seconds, but still left a bit of food on her plate every time. I asked her why she did that.

She said, "It shows I have control over my eating."

I wrote that character into a play.

What about the people who park their vehicles just over the line in the Wal-Mart parking lot? Someone who has a lot of pens in his shirt pocket? A male who has long hair? It says a lot about that person. What kind of book bags do people carry? Most people now have knapsacks. But some people don't. What kind of knapsack do they have? We are creatures of instinct.

It doesn't matter why they do it, what matters is why you think they do it. You can always use that stuff.

I was with a group of people on a retreat. There was this guy whose first finger on his left hand moved back and forth slowly and constantly. I asked someone why the guy did that and was told that the guy was an ex-horse jockey and he had fallen off his horse, which had caused neurological damage. The funny thing about the finger was when the guy played poker and he had a good poker hand, the finger would move twice as fast and the other players would fold, knowing he had a good hand. I used a similar characteristic for a character in a play I wrote.

In the John Steinbeck play *Of Mice and Men*, the character Curley keeps one of his hands moistened with Vaseline, and he wears a glove so his hand will always be soft when he touches his wife.

When writing characters like policemen, detectives, lawyers, judges, whose objectives are usually to protect or solve a case, make sure you give them something unique to separate them from all the other cops, detectives, lawyers, and judges in scripts.

The Willem Dafoe detective character in *Boondock Saints* is a good example. He is gay, and he listens to classical music while investigating the crime scene. Or the Tom Cruise lawyer character in *A Few Good Men.* His apathy and lack of experience make him unique.

Listen to the way people talk. All your characters should sound differently. See the Pointer on "Diction or Discourse."

You can have a good play/film with strong characters but a weak plot. *The Breakfast Club* is a good example.

Theme

Number three is theme. The more I write, and the older I get, the more I realize how important theme is to a script. I used to think, oh, theme, it should be number six, the bottom of the list. Theme is not that important. But theme is very important. Theme can get your audience thinking and looking at plays and films in different ways.

Theme is not the plot. Another good word for theme is ideas. What ideas are incorporated in the script? What does the audience take away from each play or movie? Themes or ideas make an audience think.

The Lord of the Rings is full of theme: good versus evil, friendship, power, addiction, death and immortality, fate, free will, and courage.

Relate back to *Agnes of God* and *Keely and Du* in the "Protagonist/Antagonist" Pointer. Both of them are heavy with theme.

Diction or Discourse

Diction or discourse is element number four. It is the words/language each character uses; the word choices the playwright uses for each character. Each character should have his or her own way of talking. Each character in *The Lord of the Rings* has their own unique voice. Gandalf doesn't sound anything like Frodo. Keep in mind that dialogue is meant to be heard, not read. Listen to how each of the characters in the TV series *Firefly* has his or her own unique voice—from the Doctor's education diction to Kaylee's bad grammar. Remember, dialogue that talks theme is a playwright serving his or her own cause. Don't tell the theme... show it.

Remember the Asian women shipped to America as mail-order brides? The writer can't pontificate about how bad he thinks it is. He must show how these women are struggling in the horrific conditions the theme is articulating.

Another important thing to remember about dialogue is that any character who talks about what they want to do is a weak character and not worthy of being performed or even read. Characters don't talk; they take action. They don't talk about climbing the wall to save their lover; they climb the wall and try to save the lover.

When I was in graduate school, I had a reading of one of my plays in which one of the characters kept saying, "I love you," to and about the woman he loved. About halfway through the reading, every time he would say it the audience would laugh. It wasn't a comedy, and the character really loved the woman, so I was confused with the reaction.

In the feedback session that followed the reading, one of the playwriting professors said, "The guy kept saying how much he loved the woman, but he never showed it. When people love someone, they might say it, but they also show their love. They do things for the one they love that shows their love. They open doors, cook for them, or buy them flowers."

Another mentor said, "I hardly ever believe a character that says, 'I love you.'"

It was one of the most important lessons I learned about writing plays. Dialogue is not just saying words. It is doing things and saying words filled with dramatic action.

Another important aspect of dialogue to keep in mind is that it is only heard once, so make it count. An audience is following along with the character's dialogue as it is being said. Both are in the present, unlike in a novel or short story where the reader can pause at any time, reread a narrative section or some dialogue as many times as she wishes, or take as long as she'd like to think about what was just read.

Stephen Sondheim tells us that he writes his song lyrics keeping in mind that the audience only gets to hear the song/lyrics one time, so the meaning must make sense the first time it is heard.

In some translations of *The Poetics*, diction is referred to as dialogue or language. And some translations say discourse. But what is discourse? Discourse includes the action lines or stage directions in the script, along with the dialogue. It refers to dialogue and the actions the character does. Actions help define character just as well as dialogue. In fact, dialogue is an action of the character.

No-Dialogue Short Script

In my screenwriting classes, I always assign the writing of a short script (four to five pages) that has a beginning, middle, and end—without any dialogue.

The difficult thing when writing these short scripts is making sure the characters are just not talking because it is part of the assignment. Do the characters need to talk? It's an important lesson in why characters talk, but that's another Pointer. I read in an acting book that "theatre is interrupted silences." I took that to mean characters only talk when they have to, when they need to fulfill a unit objective, when something gets in their way of fulfilling their super objective. If Frodo doesn't encounter any obstacles, he marches right to the volcano, never saying a word, and throws the ring in.

But back to the no-dialogue, short scripts written as an exercise in class. One of the best was about a young man coming out of a dentist's office. He stands in front of the building, his mouth swollen and full of cotton preventing him from talking. He texts someone. "On my way home." As a beautiful young woman passes by him on the sidewalk, reading a map, something accidently falls from her purse. The young man sees it, picks it up, and starts walking after her to give the item back to her. He can only grunt for her to stop, which makes her really want to ignore him. The faster he walks after her, the faster she walks. She finally outruns him, and she dodges him at a traffic light. He gives up and starts walking back the way he came from. Both characters have objectives. She wants to get to the place she is looking for on the map. He wants to get home. An MDQ is set: Will he get the item to the young girl? And all without any dialogue.

MDQ is Major Dramatic Question—what is at stake in a script. The MDQ of *The Lord of the Rings* is: Will Frodo throw the ring in the volcano? I will be talking about MDQ in a following Pointer.

There is a short film that Danny Glover directed and acted in called *Second Line*. It is seven minutes long. There's only one word of dialogue in it. But it has all these elements, including plot, characters, and especially theme. It can be viewed online.

Another example is the beginning of *There Will Be Blood*. It goes on for a long time without any dialogue, but we learn an awful lot about plot and character.

Linguistic Opportunities in Diction

Quest for Fire is another good film that doesn't have much dialogue but has a strong plot through discourse. The dialogue in the film was the creation of Anthony Burgess, a writer and linguist, illustrating that diction doesn't have to be English or any other language of the world. In *The Lord of the Rings* trilogy, Tolkien made up diction for some of the characters. In *Game of Thrones*, there's an entirely different language (Dothraki) sometimes spoken. And *Star Trek* is well known for its Klingon language that characters speak, which was made up by linguists just for the series.

Remember the percentage formula I used at the beginning of the book? In writing a screenplay (75 percent action/25 percent dialogue), discourse would be a better word because it includes the action. You could probably have a play with no dialogue, but I think it would be more difficult to write than a film with no dialogue. You need something to tell the story, whether it's action or dialogue. Talking is an action.

All the examples in the Diction and Discourse section also have something called PASTO, which we'll talk about later.

Examples of Characters with Good Diction

Again, all the classic scripts are going to have good diction. If a script has good characters, the diction is going to be good too. Willy Loman in *Death of a Salesman* is a great example of a character with very good diction. All the characters in *Death of a Salesman* have good diction.

Another example of well-written diction is the character of Jesus in *Godspell*. House in the TV show *House* and Sherlock in the series *Elementary* are two brilliant examples of characters with good diction.

The fact that Silent Bob doesn't speak in Kevin Smith's films *Clerks, Mallrats,* and *Jay and Silent Bob Strike Back* is a good example of good diction because of the looks the character gives to comment on things.

Music

Music is the next key element. When Aristotle was writing about music in *The Poetics*, he meant the twelve to fifteen men (the chorus) in robes and masks actually singing, chanting, and commenting on the action in the Greek plays. See Woody Allen's film *Mighty Aphrodite* for a wonderful example of a Greek chorus in action. In the film, we see modern characters, then he switches scenes to an ancient chorus dancing and singing in the ruins of the Teatro Greco (Greek Amphitheater). It's interesting.

By including music as one of the key elements, Aristotle meant that there should be singing in the shows. In today's scripts, music means more than singing and chanting.

Musicality of Language

In modern drama, we do not have much singing in shows (unless it is a musical), so music is linked together with the fourth element, diction. The musicality of the language becomes an element. Shakespeare gets high points because of his beautiful flowing poetry.

Then you have someone like David Mamet (*American Buffalo*), who writes very sparse, clipped language, but he gets high points, too, for his musicality. Mamet's musicality is a lot different than if you read someone like Tennessee Williams (*A Streetcar Named Desire*). You read it and you think, "No one talks like that!" But when you hear it, it flows musically. It is called good heard speech. With the birth of realism, having dialogue that sounds real (heard speech) has been the playwright's main objective.

I liken modern dialogue in scripts to the metal ball in a pinball machine bouncing off the electrodes. That's how our minds work. We don't talk in complete sentences. "As I'm trying... to tell you... how we talk... I'm doing it on purpose... a little. Know what I mean?" That, to me, is realistic dialogue. It just flows. Who talks like Blanche DuBois in *A Streetcar Named Desire?* No one but Blanche!

There's a joke that illustrates the musicality of different dialogue. A bum was outside a theatre on Broadway. When the show was over, he would panhandle the patrons for money. An elderly man and his wife dressed in evening wear were exiting the theatre, and the bum approached them.

"Do you got any spare change?" the bum asked.

"Neither a borrower or a lender be. William Shakespeare," the elderly man replied.

"Oh yeah, fuck you. David Mamet," the bum retorted.

Note the difference in the musicality between the bum's diction and the elderly man's.

Eugene O'Neil tried to capture the vernacular of several different regions of America with the way he wrote his dialogue. Read *Desire Under The Elms* or *The Iceman Cometh,* and you'll understand what I mean. He tries to capture in his writing the way people talk from those regions.

Do you need to do that? If you read a Stephen King novel set in Maine, he doesn't write in the dialect of the locals, but when you see a King film, the characters from Maine talk with that regional accent.

Should you write the vernacular or leave it up to the actors? That is something you should decide.

As Shakespeare did, Maxwell Anderson chose to write his dialogue in poetic form. Read *Winterset* to understand what I am talking about here. His poetic form is believable dialogue, but if we study it, we realize people don't talk that way. But, as a piece of theatre, we accept it as real.

Harold Pinter is another playwright who has captured the essence of heard speech. He also adds the element of not talking as part of his dialogue. Pauses can also be part of the musicality of diction. Pinter uses the pause quite a bit and very effectively in his plays. Here are two people talking in Pinter style.

GIRL

Did you do it?

(Long pause)

BOY

No.

That long pause says a lot, especially with that kind of question and answer.

In the film *The Assassination of Jesse James by the Coward Robert Ford*, Brad Pitt said he incorporated the pause into his character, Jesse James, on purpose. When you ask people something, and they don't answer right away, it says a lot about their answer. Or if they ask you something and you don't answer right away, it can make them squirm. The pause can be very effective.

It all falls under the musicality of the diction/ language.

Tempo

Another way to look at musicality is tempo. The clipped speech of Mamet has a much faster tempo than Pinter and his pause-filled dialogue. Both playwrights have their own tempo style, but their plays also vary in tempo.

If a script has all one tempo, eventually one stops hearing the dialogue. It's like driving down the Interstate at eighty miles an hour; eventually the white lines in the highway disappear.

Tempo usually changes along with the unit changes. Take any horror film and note that right before Freddy or Jason jumps out and starts killing, the tempo is usually slow, like gently rolling hills. When the killing is taking place, the tempo is fast and choppy like a lie-detector needle going haywire. Then once the killing is over, the tempo goes back to slow, gently rolling hills.

Hollywood and Music

Hollywood has taken Aristotle's fifth element of music to mean the background music that plays under a scene in a film. It can be very effective as it supports the subtext of the scene. Watch a scene in a movie with the sound off, and then watch it again with the music playing loudly. Aristotle would give music high points in Hollywood.

Spectacle

The last of the six key elements is spectacle. Aristotle said spectacle refers to the visual elements of the production. It includes lighting, even though they didn't have electric lights like we do today. What else? Costumes, sets, props, sound maybe. Sound is not visual, I know. But the technical elements of the piece make up the spectacle.

In Hollywood, they have taken spectacle to mean bombs blowing up, car chases, and other special effects. *Transformers,* or any Michael Bay film, is a great example. Yeah, he's really into spectacle.

In television, the rule is a shot shouldn't last for more than three seconds. That means the shot will change somewhere after you count to two. It'll cut, fade slowly, fade quickly, pan, etc. All that is a part of spectacle.

That part of spectacle has changed over the years. This story illustrates what I mean. When we got to the section on Musical Theatre in a Theatre Appreciation class I was teaching, I planned to show the film *Chicago.* I didn't have a copy of *Chicago,* but a student in the class did and he said he would bring it to the next class. The day I was going to show *Chicago,* I grabbed a copy of *West Side Story* from my DVD collection just in case the student forgot to bring *Chicago.* And when I showed up to class that day, the student had, indeed, forgotten to bring *Chicago,* so I began to show the class *West Side Story.* I happen to love *West Side Story* and, back in 1961, it won ten Academy Awards, including Best Picture, but the class was so restless that within twenty minutes I stopped the film. The next class I played the first twenty minutes of *Chicago* and the class loved it. We discussed the reasons they liked *Chicago* over *West Side Story* and it was all about the editing, the spectacle of the piece.

There is play titled *A Coupla White Chicks Sitting Around Talking* by John Ford Noonan, and just as the title suggests, it is about two white women, drinking coffee in a kitchen, and sitting around talking. There are no bombs going off, but according to Aristotle's definition, it has its own spectacle: set, costumes, props, and lighting. They all help tell story.

Do all scripts have these six elements? No. The classics do, like *Casablanca, The Wizard of Oz, The Lord of the Rings, Citizen Kane, Hamlet, Death of a Salesman,* or *Cat on a Hot Tin Roof.* Try to incorporate all six elements in all the scripts that you write and it will pay off.

Rough Scenario

A good practice to get into before beginning to write a script is get into the habit of completing a rough scenario. You can begin to write without answering the basic questions of a rough scenario, but using one helps make sure you have answers to the six key elements. Dr. Jerry L. Crawford composed this rough scenario list.

Seminal or Germinal Idea:

"I want to write a play about." (Example: "I want to write a play about the strange love relationship between a mother and daughter in which the mother physically abuses the daughter.")

Working Title:

Metaphorical titles are usually better than literal ones, but it is a variable. (Example: Literal–*The Private War of Susan and Jean*; Metaphorical–*The Sparrow and the Pip*.)

Form:

Is the play intended to be a comedy or a serious drama? A derivation of one or an eclectic mix of both? (Example: The play is intended to be a serious drama with minor comic interpolations.)

Style:

Based on its form, what kind or type of treatment will be given the play relative to style? (Example: Realism with expressionistic memory "flashbacks.")

Language:

Will the play be written in prose? Verse? Dialects? (Example: Realistic prose with heightened, poetic images; no dialects; Midwestern, contemporary American speech.)

Central Characters:

Include a clarification of the central DRIVE or SPINE of this character relative to what he or she wants above all else. (Example: Susan, the mother, is the central character. Her main drive is to absolve her guilt over what she did to her daughter as a child and win her daughter's love again.) Central character is also called "protagonist."

Main Opponent/Antagonist

Obstacle to the central character. (Example: Jean, the daughter, is the main opponent to her mother; Jean's main drive is to seek revenge upon her mother for the physical and psychic damage inflicted upon her by her mother.) Again note that it is a good idea to list the main drive of the antagonist as well as the protagonist; usually, those drives create a direct conflict.

Other major characters (with a brief description of them and their main drive): Example: Carl, a bartender and ex-husband to Susan; his main drive is to support his daughter–he has no idea that Susan had abused Jean.

Identify central conflict:

Identify your central conflict in one sentence. Example: A mother's guilt and love motivate her to take a job in a college counseling office where her daughter is a graduate student assistant–the daughter tries to get her mother fired while the mother tries to win back her daughter's love.

Restate the central conflict as an MDQ (major dramatic question):

Example: "Will the mother and daughter overcome their miseries and conflict and construct a new and healthy relationship?"

Major Crisis:

Briefly describe the major crisis and/or climax which resolves the conflict and answers the MDQ. Example: "The truth about the abuse is made public, the mother is fired, but in the ensuing confrontations, the daughter's revenge gives way to love."

Theme:

State the essential meaning of the play as a theme in a complete sentence. Example: "The love between a mother and daughter can ultimately overcome the deepest and worst injuries."

IMPORTANT NOTE: "The Rough Scenario" is intended strictly as a motivation and organizing tool and not as a formula or prescriptive device! If some points are not known or clear to you at the initial creation of a scenario, leave them blank or merely sketch in your impressions. Even when fully created, never use a scenario as a rigid plan. The actual writing often moves in new and fresh directions through discovery and through character fruition. Nonetheless, "The Rough Scenario" can greatly assist you with fundamental structure and what is called, "stage worthiness." When it comes time to write, a writer does so with or without such a scenario.

Exercise: Key Elements

THEME
What are the themes in *The Wizard of Oz?* Have the class name any play or film and discuss the themes found in them. Every script has themes.

TEMPO
Take the first scene of *Hamlet,* break it into units and make a chart illustrating the tempo of each unit. The visual will show you how much tempo changes in a script.

KEY ELEMENTS
As an exercise, make a list of plays or films that are strong in plot. What do you think has a strong plot? It may not have a good theme, but it has a good plot. Here's one with a good plot: *A Few Good Men.* List five more.

I guarantee if a script has a good plot, it will have good characters too. That's not necessarily true about a play or film with strong characters having a good plot. For example, a film that is strong in characters is *The Breakfast Club,* but the plot is not that strong. *Pride and Prejudice* is another. Name five more.

How about theme? Any Oliver Stone movie has a good theme. *JFK* is nothing but theme. *Wall Street* has theme, as does *Platoon.* Can you name five more?

Diction? Any Quentin Tarantino film has delightful diction. He can write wonderful scenes, like in *Inglorious Bastards* with the people hiding under the floorboards in the kitchen or the scene in the basement bar where he is ordering the three beers the "American way." Name five other plays or films with good diction.

When thinking of scripts that use music effectively, *Moulin Rouge* or *Sweeney Todd* come to mind. They are using song as Aristotle intended, but films use underscoring wonderfully too. Can you make a list of both kinds?

Die Hard or any action movie opens up with a good spectacle. I am sure a list of good scripts with spectacle in them is the easiest list to make.

ROUGH SCENARIO

Pick one of your favorite plays or films and use it to answer the questions in the Rough Scenario. Now do it for a script you have already written and then for one you intend to write.

CHAPTER 6

Four Components of Play Structure

Aristotle had another list in *The Poetics*. It is the four components of structure. The first one is exposition. Next is conflict. Then there are climax and denouement. Aristotle writes that for a script to be structurally sound, you need to have exposition, conflict, climax, and denouement.

There is a modern playwriting structural theory called PASTO. It is an acronym for the words preparation, attack, struggle, turn, and outcome. It's saying the same thing as Aristotle's four components (exposition, conflict, climax, and denouement).

The following is taken from an article I wrote for a magazine explaining and comparing Aristotle and PASTO.

PASTO

We know Aristotle as a philosopher, but he is also recognized as The Father of Theatre Criticism. Many theatre scholars and dramaturges consider his book, *The Poetics*, the bible of playwriting. His "Six Key Elements of Drama" is a very helpful tool in analyzing what makes a play work. It is his "Four Components of Play Structure," however, that I believe spawned a modern playwriting structural theory known as PASTO.

Many beginning playwrights struggle with structure when writing plays. Following the simple PASTO structure technique will help budding playwrights with this problem. A sound structure gives the play a solid foundation upon which to build.

According to Aristotle, for a play to be structurally sound, it must have these four components:

1. Exposition
2. Conflict
3. Climax
4. Denouement

That is a very workable formula. Introduce your characters and their problems (exposition), let them fight it out (conflict), allow the problems to come to a head (climax), and wrap up the loose ends (denouement).

Just as the Greeks loved their *Poetics*, modern playwrights will love their PASTO. PASTO is an acronym for a contemporary playwriting structural theory that was first introduced in a now out-of-print book, *Primer of Playwriting* by Kenneth MacGowan.

The PASTO theory was driven into me and the other student playwrights while in the MFA. playwriting program at The University of Nevada, Las Vegas, and I believe it aligns itself with Aristotle's four components of structure. It is best illustrated by this comparison:

Exposition	Preparation
	Attack
Conflict	Struggle
Climax	Turn
Denoument	Outcome

Exposition

Preparation is the introduction of the five Ws (who, what, when, where, why) that all plays must have.

It was a common practice in older plays to deliver most of the exposition of the play at the beginning of the first scene. This strategy was often done by what was called a "feather duster" scene. The maid is dusting the library in a big mansion as the butler stands in the doorway, listening to the maid say, "The master is coming home this afternoon from his holiday and he is bringing the mistress with him. The Missus is returning early from her holiday. The fireworks should begin when they all arrive."

The maid could also be talking on the telephone saying the same thing, and it would accomplish the same expositional purpose.

In today's playwriting, a large portion of the exposition is delivered in the first scene, but it all does not have to be said then. It can be delivered throughout the play.

Exposition–preparation is needed to set the play's location, introduce character objectives, and relate previous action.

Attack

The Attack is why I like PASTO over Aristotle. It is an added fifth component. The attack is the moment the playwright has set the play in motion, established what is at stake in the play, when the audience knows why they are sitting in their seats, or when the MDQ (Major Dramatic Question) is asked. Without an MDQ, the audience loses interest in the play.

In Greek plays or those plays with five acts, like Shakespeare or Moliere, the MDQ was always asked at the end of the first act.

Take *Romeo and Juliet* for example. Scene One opens with the fight between members of the Montague and Capulet families. There is a question asked there. Will the feud ever end? But it is not the major dramatic question.

Scene One offers two other questions. Lord and Lady Montague ask Benvolio what is wrong with their son, Romeo. But again it is not the MDQ. Next

Benvolio asks Romeo why he is acting so strangely. Romeo says he is unhappy with his latest girlfriend, Rosaline, posing another question: Will Romeo find another girlfriend? But that's still not the MDQ.

Scene Two opens with Lord Capulet and Paris, as the latter asks for Juliet's hand in marriage. And here is another question.

Scene Three shifts to Lady Capulet, the nurse, and Juliet. Juliet's mother asks her daughter if she is ready to be married. A big question but not the MDQ.

In Scene Four, Romeo and his friends decide they should crash the Capulet party being held that night so they can all meet some new girls. More questions asked but not the MDQ.

At the Capulet party in Scene Five, Romeo and Juliet meet, fall in love, and at the end of Scene Five, which is the end of the first act, Juliet asks the nurse to find out what Romeo's name is. The nurse tells Juliet that he is a Montague, the son of the family's enemy–thus setting the MDQ of the show: Will Romeo and Juliet's love survive?

Check out the MDQ at the end of the first act of *Hamlet*. Will Hamlet avenge his father's death?

In modern playwriting, the theory is to ask the MDQ early on in the script. In Julie Jensen's playwriting book, *Brief and Brilliant*, she states that the "MDQ should be asked by the 10 percent point in the script."

Conflict/Struggle

Conflict–Struggle, the protagonist tries to accomplish the super objective, often connected to the MDQ, and is opposed by the antagonist trying to stop the central character from accomplishing the super objective, producing conflict. The core of all plays is conflict. All the events that happen on the way to answering the MDQ are the conflict or struggle.

As I was giving this Pointer in a playwriting class, a student asked, "So there is more than one struggle?" And indeed there are, so I began adding an *S* to the word struggle and I like it–struggles.

Climax – Turn

The turn occurs when the MDQ has been answered. Do not confuse turn with turning point. There are many turning points in a play, but only one turn or answer to the MDQ.

Denoument

After the MDQ has been answered, there is Denouement–Outcome. There is nothing to keep the audience engaged in the play, so wrap up the loose ends and end the play as quickly as you can.

Plays that continue to try to tell the story after the MDQ has been answered usually just bore the audience. I wrote an adaptation of *The Three Little Pigs* that had a "Where Are They Now" monologue after the climax of defeating the Big Bad Wolf. At the morning premiere performance, as the narrator told the audience what each character was doing now, the children in the audience were so restless that almost none of the last monologue was even heard. I did a rewrite of the ending before the afternoon performance, cutting the ending monologue down to just a couple of lines, and the children left the second performance with the happy feeling they had after the climax had occurred.

There are times when you can get away with a long denouement–outcome. The final film of *The Lord of the Rings* trilogy is a good example. Once Frodo throws the ring in the volcano, the MDQ has been answered, and there is a climax. The film continues for twenty more minutes, but the audience is so invested in the show and its characters that the long outcome works.

But generally the rule is to wrap things up as quickly as possible after the MDQ has been answered.

Using PASTO, I will now break down The *Wizard of Oz.*

In the Preparation, Dorothy, a thirteen or fourteen-year-old girl, lives on a farm in Kansas with her aunt and uncle. It is spring, and three farmhands work on the farm. Dorothy has a dog, Toto, who has just bitten an evil-acting woman.

Most people think the Attack or MDQ is: Will Dorothy find her way home? Actually, that happens too late in the story. The MDQ is set earlier when Dorothy sings "Over the Rainbow." The MDQ is: Will she find a better place to live?

The Struggles are plenty. They begin when Dorothy decides to run away because her dog has been taken away. She meets the gypsy, she has to get back home, she lands in Oz, she faces the Wicked Witch making her life difficult, she has to get to the Emerald City, and she has to get the Witch's broom. Even trying to pick apples from the trees because she is hungry and the trees will not let her is a struggle. Crossing the poppy field is a struggle. The struggles make up most of the play.

The Turn happens when she is clicking her heels together saying, "There's no place like home," actually answering the MDQ: Will Dorothy find a better place to live? And when she gets home, she realizes she does not need to find a better place to live.

The Outcome is very short. Dorothy says the others in her life were with her all along, even in the other world, and "There's no place like home."

All plays share the same blueprint, and PASTO is a solid test to make sure your play is structurally sound. I think Aristotle would approve of PASTO, and if he could write a second edition of *The Poetics*, I am sure he would add the Attack to his components of play structure.

Examples of MDQs Set Early in a Script

Here are the beginnings of two plays of mine where the MDQ is set early in the script. The first is a forty-five to fifty-minute play titled *The Great Santa Claus Reindeer Roundup* published by Brooklyn Publishers.

SCENE ONE

> (AT RISE: SANTA is
> discovered by his sleigh.
> He is lifting a weight from
> the back of the sleigh. The
> SOUND of a pack of dogs
> barking can be heard off
> stage. FAIRBANKS, an
> Alaskan malamute, sled
> dog, enters.)

FAIRBANKS

Here, Santa, let me help you.

> (He runs to help SANTA
> lift the weight from the
> back of the sleigh.)

SANTA

Thanks, Fairbanks.

FAIRBANKS

I thought Tiny was going to help you put things away?

SANTA

He'll be here.

> (They finish lifting the
> weight.)

Why aren't you with the other dogs? You must be as
tired as they are.

FAIRBANKS

I am; but rest can wait. I just wanted to make sure that you were all right?

SANTA

Thanks, Fairbanks, you're a good dog.

FAIRBANKS

Just part of my duties as the lead sled dog. Is something bothering you?

SANTA

No, no, I'm fine. I'm just tired too.

FAIRBANKS

You were a little rough on the dog team. Remember, today was just a test run. Just making sure the sleigh is in working order. It's not been used in almost a year. Christmas Eve is two weeks away.

SANTA

I know, you and the others are a good dog sled team, and have been for many years.

FAIRBANKS

We're all Alaskan malamutes ... especially trained to pull your magic sleigh full of toys each Christmas Eve to all the good boys and girls around the world.

SANTA

It just seems like it's getting harder for the team to pull the sleigh.

FAIRBANKS
That's because each year the sleigh gets heavier and heavier.

SANTA
There are more and more toys each holiday.

FAIRBANKS
So, what are you really saying?

SANTA
Maybe we need some more dogs to pull the sleigh this Christmas?

(TINY, a tall elf, enters.)

TINY
Sorry, Santa, that I'm late. I fell asleep while I was waiting for you to get back. The practice run never takes you this long. Did you have a problem?

SANTA
We have a big problem.

TINY
Don't punish me for being late. It won't happen again. I swear.

FAIRBANKS
But will more dogs be the solution?

                    TINY
I know I'm a problem. What good is an elf as tall as me?

                    SANTA
Not you, Tiny.

                    FAIRBANKS
Maybe something other than dogs should pull your
magic sleigh.

                    SANTA
Are you suggesting we find another animal to take
your job?

                    FAIRBANKS
I hate to say it, but yes, there are stronger animals than
dogs.

                    SANTA
Maybe you're right. We'll have to find your replacements
quickly.

                    FAIRBANKS
Yes, two weeks doesn't give us a lot of time. The other
dogs and I will help train who ever you find.

                    SANTA
You're my main dog, Fairbanks.

                    FAIRBANKS
How about horses?

SANTA

No, they would make too much noise as they galloped and would wake up the children.

FAIRBANKS

Maybe elk?

SANTA

Elk might work, but do we have any elk at the North Pole?

TINY

I think it should be a dragon.

SANTA

Tiny, you read too many fantasy books.

TINY

Dragons are big and strong. It would only take one. And a fire-breathing dragon could melt the snowdrifts that slowed the sleigh down.

SANTA

Dragons have been extinct for hundreds of years.

TINY

I have a dragon friend.

FAIRBANKS

You mean you have an imaginary friend that is a dragon.

TINY

No, he's real. And since he's odd like me... he understands the problems I face.

SANTA

Tiny, I'm afraid your dragon friend would scare the children.

TINY

No, he wouldn't. His name is Dagmar. He's real friendly. And he can fly. That sure would make the ocean crossings go faster.

(MRS. CLAUS enters.)

MRS. CLAUS

There you are, my dear. I was getting worried.

SANTA

I'm sorry, Mrs. Claus. I should have let you know we were back.

(MRS and SANTA embrace.)

MRS. CLAUSE

Guess what I found by our back door this morning? A baby reindeer.

(SANTA and FAIRBANKS exchange a look.)

SANTA and FAIRBANKS

That's it.

(They slap a high five.)

Reindeer!!!

(The LIGHTS fade to
black. Music bridges the
gap between scenes.)

The script is sixty-four typed pages. The MDQ is asked on page two: Will Santa find new animals to pull the sleigh for Christmas? And by three and a half pages into the script we know he'll be searching for reindeer. Setting a time limit raised the stakes. He only has two weeks to do it.

The next script is an adaptation I wrote of Cinderella called *Cinderella and the Fairy Godfather* published by Playscripts, Inc.

SCENE ONE

(AT RISE: The stage is
empty. There is no set,
only the black curtains. A
trumpet fanfare is heard
and the PRINCE enters
and holds up a glass
slipper.)

PRINCE

I am the Prince of this kingdom and I must find the foot that fits this glass slipper. When I find the young lady whose foot slips into this slipper... she will be my bride and Princess.

> (PRINCE goes into the audience with the slipper. He tries it on the feet of several children in the audience. Of course it doesn't fit any of them.)

> (RAGS enter. He is a fairy godmother in training. He has a day's growth of beard and wears clothes that look more like rags. He also wears a suggestion of a tutu.)

RAGS

Excuse me. May I have your attention? Hello?
> (He shouts.)

Be quiet! Thank you.
> (To the PRINCE.)

Hey you, Prince guy. I think you're too early. Please you gotta get out of here.

PRINCE

But I must find my Princess?

RAGS

You'll find her, but not right now.

> (PRINCE gets back on
> stage.)

PRINCE

When?

RAGS

Look will you leave.

PRINCE

Who are you?

RAGS

The name is Rags, and I'm a fairy Godmother.

PRINCE

Are you dressed for some kind of masquerade party?

RAGS

Will you please leave the stage and let me do my job.

> (RAGS raises his hand/
> wand and there is a
> SOUND effect that lets
> the PRINCE know RAGS
> means business.)

PRINCE

You better not mess this up.

                    RAGS
I'll do my best.

                         (The PRINCE exits.)

                    RAGS (cont'd)
                    (To the audience.)
Hi.

                    CHILDREN
Hi.

                    RAGS
Oh boy. I think I'm in big trouble.
                         (He talks to himself.)
Relax.
                         (To the children.)
Hello.

                    CHILDREN
Hello.

                    RAGS
We already said that, didn't we? I'm sorry. I'm a little
nervous and confused. You see I'm supposed to be a
Fairy Godmother, but as you can see I'm not much in
the Godmother department. I'm more of a Godfather.
                    (Does a Marlin Brando
                    impression.)
I'm gonna make you an offer you can't refuse.

> (SOUND: The Godfather
> theme is heard briefly.
> He speaks in his normal
> voice.)

You see, there ain't many Godfather jobs around. I've been waiting so long for one that my clothes have rotted, and that's how I got my nickname, Rags. But, I waited patiently all this time for my first assignment. There's a shortage of Godmothers so I volunteered for this assignment. Godmother I ain't, but since I supposed to be one I found this tutu to help with the fairy part. And for my first God mothering duty I'm supposed to help this young girl named... a... her name is? Sleeping Beauty. No, that not it.

CHILDREN
Cinderella.

RAGS
That's right, and I think she marries a prince? Is that right?

CHILDREN
Yes.

RAGS
All right. You're all a big help. Thanks. Hey, I think you can help me a lot. You see, sometimes I get so excited I can't think straight. If that happens, you can help me. Will you do that?

                    CHILDREN
Yes.

                    RAGS
When I get too excited I will ask you, "What do I do?"
and you tell me, "relax." Can you remember that?

                    CHILDREN
Yes.

                    RAGS
Let's try it. What do I do?

                    CHILDREN
Relax.

                    RAGS
I think you can do better than that. What do I do?

                    CHILDREN
Relax.

                    RAGS
That will do. I feel a lot better about this assignment
knowing that you are here to help me. Now, as a fairy
Godmother I am supposed to help who?

                    CHILDREN
Cinderella.

                    RAGS
And who does she live with?

CHILDREN
Evil stepmother and sisters.

RAGS
That's right ... an evil stepmother and was it one or two
stepsisters?

CHILDREN
Two.

RAGS
Two. Alright, here we go.
(He chants.)
One stepmother, two stepsisters, and no fellas.
I must meet and talk to the maiden Cinderella.
Show us their house ... make it come into view.
Do it now, I command, do it on my cue.
(RAGS waves his hand/
wand and the set of
the stepmother's house
appears. A magic SOUND
accompanies this. The set
was behind a black curtain
or scrim and the curtain
was raised to reveal the
set. It consists of a table
and three chairs and a
fireplace.)
Hey, this is easy, especially with your help. Thank you.
You're all helping me fulfill my dream.

(MOTHER enters.)

This script is forty-one typed pages. The MDQ is set on page one. Will the Prince find the foot that fits the slipper? I have found in adapting fairy tales that the MDQ in the written fairy tale is never at the beginning of the story but toward the end. In keeping with the 10 percent rule, you must find a way to move that question to the beginning of the play so the script has something at stake early. That is what I have done with *Cinderella and the Fairy Godfather.*

Don't Overwrite After the Climax Has Been Reached

Remember I discussed the play *Keely and Du,* and it centers its MDQ on the abortion issue with the MDQ "Will she have the baby?" She keeps saying, "I can do whatever I want with my body!" Toward the end of the script, it's the young girl's birthday. To celebrate the birthday, the nurse brings in a dress, two warm beers, and a radio. She lets the young girl put the dress on to celebrate her birthday because she's been in hospital garb the whole time. They drink the beer, turn the radio on, and dance around. Then the two abductors come in and say, "What is going on here?" The young girl runs to the bed and grabs the coat hanger (which the dress was brought in on) and aborts herself right then. It's a hell of a climactic moment. You don't see it happen. As she grabs the wire hanger, the stage is flooded in a wash of red light for a beat and then goes to black very quickly. You just know what happened.

After that climactic moment, there is a scene where Du has had a stroke and is in a nursing home, and Keely comes to take care of her. I believe the play is over. The

MDQ has been answered, so wrap up the loose ends with the denouement. I think this denouement scene goes on too long.

Don't forget the example of my long denouement that was cut from my adaptation of *The Three Little Pigs*.

However, sometimes a long denouement works. The ending denouement of *The Lord of the Rings* goes on for twenty minutes or more after Frodo has thrown the ring into the volcano. It works here because we are so invested in all the characters that we want to know what happened to them all.

No New Information in the Denouement

In my never-ending quest to earn my $17.3 million salary, let me mention one last thing about denouement: Do not add new information in the denouement.

A student mentioned that in *Blade Runner* directed by Ridley Scott, new information was revealed in the denouement about whether or not the character was human. I would like to elucidate on that. The information given in that example is not new information. It is an answer to something that was set up earlier in the film.

Had it been introduced to the audience earlier in the film, then it is not surprise masquerading as some sort of climax.

I find that many beginning scriptwriters think that some big twist at the end of the script qualifies as climax, and it doesn't. The key is: How do you foreshadow the big twist so that when it is revealed at the end, it is not a surprise but a revelation? It is done really well in *The Sixth Sense.*

Exercise: Setting an MDQ

Write several three- to five-page scenes that set an MDQ. Do not use more than three characters and one locale, giving each character a strong super objective.

CHAPTER 7

Top Ten Mistakes Beginning Playwrights Make

"A novel it's different. It's kind of exhilarating not to have to cut to the bone constantly. Oh, well I can go over here for a moment. I can say what I think the guy was thinking or what the day looked like or what the bird was doing. If you do that as a play-wright, you're dead." David Mamet[1]

Writing plays is very different from writing short stories or novels. Some writers say it is more difficult because the plot must all be told with dialogue. There are no descriptive passages in drama to tell the story. The actions the actors take and the design elements can help tell a story, but they are dictated by what the playwright writes.

Novel writing is an examination of one's own emotional state and mental processes (what someone thinks). That is why novels are usually written in past

---

1 Mamet, David. *The Paris Review*, Spring 1997.

tense. Scripts are always written in present tense, even in a flashback, it is played in present tense.

An entire article could be written on that quandary (novel writing vs. scriptwriting), as it is probably the number one problem facing all playwrights. But beginning playwrights encounter other problems too. And here is my top ten list.

1. They Don't Use Proper Playwriting Format

When reading a play in a textbook, a book, or even the acting editions the play publishers sell, it is not typed in the proper playwriting format. It looks like this:

BOB: Do you know the proper way to format a play?

CATHY: Here, let's look at the book I use in my drama class.

BOB: Good idea.

This is not the proper way to format a play. Some use this format to cut down on pages and thus cut publishing costs. Proper play formatting uses a lot of space on the page, and that adds to the total page count. See Chapter 8 on Proper Formatting.

2. They Write Film Scripts, Not Plays

Because most beginning writers of plays are so rooted in television and film, they think that way when they write a play. Most see many more films and watch a lot more television than go to the theatre to see a live play.

Plays can put two characters in a room and let them go at each other. There doesn't need to be multiple scenes in a play. There can be, but plays develop longer scenes between the characters than film does.

The nature of films is movement. After all, films are called motion pictures. Film likes to show off the ease of changing from one scene to another.

Television is even faster paced than film in terms of changing locales or shots. Think of how quickly music videos move. The rule of thumb in TV is a shot doesn't last more than three seconds.

The ease of changing locale in TV or film can't be matched on the stage, but beginning playwrights continue to draw from TV and film and write multiple scenes that cannot be carried out easily onstage. For instance, shifting from inside a bedroom to a beach scene. Or they write locations, like a used car lot, that are not feasible onstage. How would a set designer get all the cars on a stage? Or change scenery from a bedroom to a beach quickly?

3. They Don't Realize That Settings for Plays Don't Have to be as Realistic as Film and Television

Films and television rely on realistic scenery. They can take the audience to places they have never been and make them feel like they are right there, especially with 3D.

A good scene designer for the theatre can make a set very realistic too. But in the theatre, audiences accept nonrealistic scenery. A set doesn't have to reflect reality. Unit sets are used in many productions where the set pieces become anything the play tells the audience it is.

Or in the case of a play I wrote called *The Way the World Turns* where only six, two-foot square boxes become anything they needed to be, from two chairs beside two end tables, to a counter at a Burger King, to the Pearly Gates of Heaven.

That sort of thing would never work in film or TV because the audience has come to expect realism. But because beginning playwrights are thinking film, they think everything must be real. In fact, anything can be suggested, even props.

There is a 2007 production of Stephen Sondheim's *Company* directed by John Doyle that illustrates this theory very effectively. The set was very minimal, with only a couple of Plexiglas cubes permanently placed onstage that became whatever they needed them to become in the different scenes (chair, table). The grand piano that was on the stage became everything from a park bench to a bed. And very few props were used. There were glasses that were used to drink from, but there wasn't any liquid in them.

Remember, Shakespeare didn't have any scenery. He told the audience where they were in his dialogue and they believed it. The play *Our Town* was written to be performed without a set. Audiences will accept suggestions of scenery in plays more than in film.

4. They Don't Make Today Unique

Plays are not written about ordinary people in ordinary situations. They might seem ordinary, but that is because we can relate to the characters and the situations they are in, as though their everyday lives are unfolding in front of an audience onstage. But in plays, there is something unique about their everyday lives that make the events of their lives take on a new shape.

What is that unique factor?

The ghost in *Hamlet* sets that day apart from any other Prince Hamlet has lived. Dorothy finally decides to leave the farm in *The Wizard of Oz*, which also happens to be a day a tornado hits. In *Oedipus*, the plague has become unbearable.

In David Ball's book *Backwards and Forwards* he says, "Playwrights rarely create people living out just another day in their lives. Something out of the ordinary arises– usually but not always early in the play–and that causes a turn from ordinary events, a turn the rest of the play follows."[2]

5. They Write Too Much Plot in the Stage Directions

Here is the opening of a play:

SCENE ONE
(AT RISE: LORIE, a
senior in high school, with
strawberry blond hair, and

---

2 David Ball, *Backwards and Forwards: A Technical Manual for Reading Plays.* Carbondale: Southern Illinois University Press, 1983.

green eyes is discovered in
her bedroom sitting on her
bed, crying. She has been
fighting with her father for
the past two months since
a drunk driver killed her
mother in an automobile
accident. She is taking
out the fact that she is
angry about her mother's
death and her missing her
mother on her father. Her
father, JAMES, enters
her bedroom without
knocking.)

LORIE

How many times do I have to ask you to knock before
you come in?

(JAMES has taken to
drinking since his wife's
death, he has lost his job
at the local paper mill, and
he hasn't shaved or taken a
bath in days.)

A very melodramatic scene but written that way
to prove a point. There is a lot of plot information
included in the above stage directions. Lorie is a senior
in high school, she has strawberry blond hair, she is in
her bedroom, her mother was just killed by a drunk

driver, and she is taking out her frustrations on her father. James is now drinking and used to work at the paper mill and he is unkempt.

All these facts can be very helpful to the actors playing the parts as they help develop their characters.

But if any of that information is important and the audience needs to know it–they won't learn any of it unless it is said in the dialogue. Yes, we can see that Lorie is in a bedroom, but we don't know whose bedroom it is. We can see that she is crying, but we won't know why she is crying–a drunk driver killed her mother. Just as we won't know that James looks the way he does because he has taken to drinking and the drinking has made him lose his job.

If something is important and the audience needs to know it–put it in the dialogue.

"I think that as a playwright, if I detail that environment, then I'm taking away something from [the designers]. I'm taking away their creativity and their ability to have input themselves, not just to follow what the playwright has written. So I do a minimum set description and let the designers create within that." (August Wilson)[3]

6. They Make All the Character Voices Sound the Same

Characters in plays are as different as people are in real life. Just as characters in every play have their own objective, they need their own voice, too.

---

3 Wilson, August. African American Review, Spring 2001.

The characters in many beginning playwrights' plays all sound the same, and that is because the dialogue is coming from the same writer. The characters all sound like the playwright.

Make sure you give characters a life of their own and strong super objectives. In doing so, you will give them a unique voice.

Many times when writers dash out a first draft of a play, they are concentrating on plot and thus all the characters will sound the same. They know what the character is going to say and the dialogue word choices, so they quickly write the play, giving it a beginning, middle, and end.

It's then very easy to go back in a second draft and give each character a unique voice. Let's say that a character is a sports fanatic; he loves all kinds of sports. In a first draft, a friend could ask him if he wants to go to the store. He replies, "yes."

In a second draft, the same friend asks if he wants to go to the store, and he replies, "that would be better than catching my limit in sunfish." The response illustrates the character's love for sports and fishing.

Learn from the classics. Read *A Streetcar Named Desire* and note how none of the characters in that play sound the same. Blanche sounds different not only from Stanley (of course she would) but Stella too. Stanley sounds different from Mitch, and Eunice and Steve sound different from Stanley and Stella.

Can you distinguish the different voices of the characters in your scripts? Of course they will sound different when actors are reading them. Can you tell the difference in them by reading them silently?

7. They Give Only One Character an Objective in Most Scenes

Most beginning playwrights have one character with a strong objective in a two-person scene and the other character doesn't have an objective at all. They become a sounding board for the character with the strong objective. Remember an earlier Pointer where I called it playing Ed McMahon to Johnny Carson on *The Tonight Show*. See the Chapter Two Pointer, A Taxi Diver and Me, for an example.

"People only speak to get something. If I say, Let me tell you a few things about myself, already your defenses go up; you go, Look, I wonder what he wants from me, because no one ever speaks except to obtain an objective. That's the only reason anyone ever opens his or her mouth, onstage or offstage. They may use a language that seems revealing, but if so, it's just coincidence, because what they're trying to do is accomplish an objective." (David Mamet)[4]

8. An MDQ is Not Firmly Set

I spoke earlier about the MDQ (Major Dramatic Question), "Aristotle Meets PASTO: A Quick and Easy Lesson in Playwriting Structure," but here is a quick review.

It is the point when the "what is at stake" in the play is set. What the audience is waiting for (the climax) in

---

4 Mamet, David. *The Paris Review*, Spring 1997.

the play. Why the audience is even interested in the play. All plays have one.

In *Death of a Salesman*, it is: Will Willy be able to provide for Biff? In *Oklahoma*: Will Curley and Laurie get together? *Hamlet*: Will Hamlet avenge his father's death?

Because beginning playwrights know the end of the play, they often forget to set up the MDQ at the beginning of the play. Or they get started with the plot so quickly that they forget to tell the audience what is at stake. Some just want to be mysterious, and they don't want to be blatant about what their play is about, and that only goes so far when the audience discovers there is nothing at stake.

When should the MDQ be asked in a play?

In modern playwriting, the MDQ should be firmly set by the 10 percent point. The audience needs to know early to understand what is at stake and to root for the MDQ satisfaction.

As I mentioned earlier, most people think the MDQ of *The Wizard of Oz* is: Will Dorothy find her way out of Oz and get back home? But that's not it. That question is asked too late in the script to be the MDQ. The MDQ in *The Wizard of Oz* is: Will Dorothy find a better place to live? And it's set in the song, "Somewhere Over the Rainbow."

The MDQ in *Pippin* is: Will Pippin find something to satisfy him in his life? And it is set in the song, "Corner of the Sky."

Both songs are sung and set the MDQ firmly around the 10 percent point in each script. Here is some trivia about musicals — the MDQ in a musical is usually set in the first or second song in the show.

9. They Don't Make the Climax an Event

The climax should be the highest emotional moment for both the characters in the play and the audience watching the play.

All the characters in the play are trying to fulfill their super objective. The protagonist is fighting to fulfill his objective and answer the MDQ. Many times inexperienced playwrights will answer the MDQ with a sentence or two, telling us the problem has been solved. Remember it is always better to show and not tell. Answer the MDQ with an event. An event should illustrate the climax of the play. Frodo throwing the ring into the volcano is an event.

In *The Wizard of Oz*, Dorothy doesn't get to go home in the balloon with the Wizard, and it looks like she will never get home or find a better place to live. But the Good Witch saves the day when she tells Dorothy to click her heels together and she will make it home. That is a classic event. Dorothy even has to say, "there's no place like home," as she is clicking her heels, answering the MDQ when she is transported home that there is no better place to live than where she is.

In *A Streetcar Named Desire*, the climax is Stanley's rape of Blanche, even though the event is not shown, the lead up to it strongly suggests the event took place.

10. They Think that Death is the Ultimate Climax

Yes, death is an event, especially if it is the result of a sword fight as in *Hamlet*, and it is a very big climax. There is nothing bigger, but it is not always the best choice for climax. If I had a dollar for every play written in my classes that ended with death, I'd be a very rich teacher.

There are better ways to end a script than with death. Guns banging, swords clashing, or bombs blowing up all are very loud and seem very climactic. Having to live with your foe after a major climactic moment can be more dramatic than killing them.

The Willy and Biff climactic scene at the end of *Death of a Salesman* is a great illustration. Yes, ultimately Willy does commit suicide (it is not shown), but the climactic scene that leads up to that is full of truth and love that both characters have been avoiding for years.

11. A Few Other Mistakes

I know the title of this piece is Top Ten Mistakes Beginning Playwrights Make, so what is this number eleven? The title wouldn't have sounded as good if it was Top Eleven and there are a few other things that needed to be put in this article.

Write it and don't worry about how it will be done.

You are a playwright, not a designer or director. They pay directors and designers to figure out how to stage what you have written.

My thesis play in graduate school was called *The Clown, the Penguin, and the Princess*, a fantasy about how alcohol moves from one generation to the next. The script had characters flying in several scenes. When writing, I saw the characters flying just as Peter did in *Peter Pan*. The original production didn't have a budget to allow for that. The directors and designers solved the problem by having the characters stand on a piece of furniture when flying. The actors held out their hands like wings on an airplane, they were lit from the chest up in a green light, and Stravinsky music was played. It worked better than if they had flown in *Peter Pan*.

Look at set designs for *Les Miserables* (John Napier) or *Phantom of the Opera* (Maria Bjornson). You write it – let the director and designers worry about how it will be done. Each show's set demands called for numerous locations on a grand scale and in each show the scenery designs were spectacular.

Characters don't talk—they do.

The first thing you have to know about playwriting is that any character who talks about what they want to do is a weak character and not worthy of being performed or even read. Characters don't talk; they take action. They don't talk about climbing the wall to save their lover; they climb the wall and try to save the lover. A character doesn't talk about swimming the moat to enter the castle. He jumps in and swims because he is driven by objectives and must fulfill his objective like it was a desperate quest.

Characters in plays are not real people; they don't procrastinate like people in real life do. They find themselves in a situation and they fight to get out, or relieve themselves from the pressure.

Dialogue is not just words, but words that are filled with action. And not just any action, but dramatic action.

What is the difference between action and dramatic action? Action is activity and dramatic action is activity with a purpose.

All characters try desperately to fulfill a purpose through the actions they take. They might be sidetracked by another character's purpose, but they always try to fulfill their own purpose first.

They forget that plays are written in real time.

For every second that ticks off for the characters in their situations onstage–the same amount of time is ticking off for the audience watching the play. Plays are written in real time.

Yes, you can have a blackout and have the lights come up ten seconds, minutes, hours, or years later, but once the scene begins, it is played in real time once again.

Film can change time. It is called film time. It was first used in a film called *Battleship Potemken* (1925). There was a crowd of people running down a very large set of stairs. In real time, it might have taken the people five seconds to run down the stairs, but in the film that five seconds was turned into thirty seconds. The shot was edited to take longer than it actually does.

You cannot slow down time in plays, even in a flashback the scene is played in real time.

CHAPTER 8

Formatting

Proper Playwriting Format

What about the playwrights who say, "Don't worry about the formatting. If the play is good it will get produced." If a script is not typed in the proper formatting, a publisher won't even read it. That is one of the first methods to weed through the thousands of manuscripts received daily.

BOB
Do you know the proper way to format a play?

CATHY
Here, let's look at the book I use in my drama class.

BOB
Good idea.

> CATHY

But what about stage directions?

> BOB

They go on the right quarter of the page.

> > (BOB holds up a
> > manuscript to show
> > CATHY what he means
> > by the right quarter of the
> > page.)

> CATHY

I see that all character names and names in stage directions are in capital letters.

> BOB

You're right, but not when a name like Cathy is written in a line of dialogue.

> CATHY

I bet we can find a computer program that has the proper formatting for plays.

> BOB
> (Laughing)

I'm way ahead of you.

> > (He types on a computer.)

There seems to be quite a few of them.

(A VOICE from the
heavens is heard. BOB and
CATHY look up.)

VOICE

This is Dionysus, Greek God of the Theatre. Be careful when using playwriting programs you get from the Internet. The ones I am familiar with are not the correct format.

BOB

What should we do?

VOICE

Most of the play publishers will send you a page that illustrates the proper formatting.

CATHY

Can you tell us if our play is going to be a hit?

VOICE

Read "The Top Ten Mistakes Beginning Playwrights Make,"and it stands a better chance of being good. It is very important to get used to typing plays in the proper format.

Play Title Pages

There are more title pages to play scripts than film scripts. They should not be included in the numbering of the actual script. Use Roman numerals at the bottom of each page. First there is the title page, then the copyright page, followed by the cast of characters page, synopsis of scenes page, and last the dedication page and/or quotes you would like to include (the dedication page is not included in the example to follow).

THE WIZARD OF BAMBOOZLEMENT

by
Bob May

Seventh Draft
May 6, 2009

©
2009
by

Bob May

All inquiries should be sent
to:

Bob May
100 United Way
Anywhere, AR 7XXXX
(501) XXX-XXXX
bmay@uca.edu

CAST OF CHARACTERS (In speaking order.)

GIDGET
FIGURE/WJ
THE QUEEN
CANDY
THE WICKED WITCH OF THE WEST
BEANIE
CLASSMATE A
CLASSMATE B
CLASSMATE C
B. J.
DOROTHY
HANSEL
GRETEL
SNOW WHITE
DEWIE DECIMAL
LEWIE DECIMAL
CHRIS
VOICE
HEWIE DECIMAL
PROFESSOR LIBRUM

SYNOPSIS OF SCENES

Scene One: The living room of Beanie and Gidget Boren, late evening.

Scene Two: The same; immediately following.

Scene Three: The garage behind the Boren Home; immediately following.

Scene Four: Someplace in Bookworld; the next morning, 6 AM.

Scene Five: A crossroad in Bookworld; 7 AM.

Scene Six: Another location in Bookworld; 8 AM.

Scene Seven: Another location in Bookworld; 10 AM.

Scene Eight: At the main library of Bookworld; 11 AM.

Scene Nine: Librum's Lair; immediately following.

Scene Ten: Outside the Wicked Witch of the West's castle; immediately following.

Scene Eleven: Inside the Wicked Witch of the West's castle; just before 12 PM, noon.

Scene Twelve: Librum's Lair; not long after.

Proper Film Formatting

Proper film formatting is the opposite of play formatting. Lines in plays are more important, they cross the entire page, and the stage directions are to the right quarter of the page. In film, formatting the action lines are more important, so they cross the entire page and the dialogue is in the center of the page. What they have in common is the character names above speaking lines are in CAPS in the center of the page on the same tab (do not use the center justification feature).

Mark Schwartz, Associate Professor of Screenwriting at the School of Film & Television at Loyola Marymount University in Los Angeles, has written a wonderful short screenplay, *Good Format Hunting*, used here with permission, in which his characters discuss proper screenwriting formatting, and at the same time the screenplay is illustrating what one looks like.

FADE IN:

EXT. ALLEYWAY – NIGHT

Blazing gunfire shatters the night.

Running for their lives, JOHN and MARTHA, both midtwenties, race into the dimly lit alleyway.

JOHN
Look out!

He grabs Martha, diving behind a dumpster as zinging bullets ricochet above their heads.

> MARTHA
> What do they want from me, John?
> What do they want?

> JOHN
> Can only be one thing.

He controls his own fear. And looks her in the eye.

> JOHN
> Standard screenplay format.

> MARTHA
> (filling with dread)
> Not that...

> JOHN
> You can do it, Martha. I swear on my
> mother's grave you can do it!

More gunfire. John holds her close. A trace of skepticism furrows her brow.

> MARTHA
> Your mother's not dead, John.

He shrugs, offering no apologies. She smirks.

MARTHA
Don't you think this is getting just a
little melodramatic, on-the-nose and
over-the-top?

JOHN
This is about format, Martha. Not
dialogue.

MARTHA
So enlighten me.

JOHN
Set your left margin at 1.5 inches and
your right margin at 1.0. Top, 1 inch
to the body and 0.5 to the number,
like the one above. Leave 0.5 to 1.5
inches on the bottom, depending on
your page break.

MARTHA
What if I am slightly off?

JOHN
Not the end of the world.

Another blast of gunfire.

MARTHA
(rolling her eyes)
Tell it to the creep with the uzi.

JOHN
I'd rather tell you about the fonts.

MARTHA
John, this is no time to talk dirty.

JOHN
I'm talking 12 pt 10 pitch Courier.

MARTHA
Ahh. But what if I wanna use boldface, colors, and italics? To make meaningful words stand out, and the script look pretty.

JOHN
Black Courier only! It's industry standard. Not a pretty thing.

MARTHA
So I gather.

John glances around. Sees a door.

JOHN
Let's go inside.

INT. CLASSROOM – NIGHT

John and Martha sneak into an otherwise deserted classroom.

MARTHA
It's good to be away from all that
gunfire.

JOHN
Don't be so sure.

MARTHA
Oh, right. We're in a classroom.

John closes steel blinds making the windows. Activates
the metal detector at the door.

MARTHA
Tell me about capitalization.

JOHN
Slug lines are always capitalized.

MARTHA
What some call scene headings.

JOHN
Right. INT. CLASSROOM – DAY.
That sort of thing. It's a good idea
to capitalize characters' names when
they're first introduced, like we were
on page one. And always put the
names of the character speaking in
caps, like mine is now.

MARTHA
Speaking of speaking, where should
the margins be set for dialogue?

JOHN
Left, 3 inches and right, 2.5, more or
less. Again, don't fret if it's a little bit
off. Tab the name of the character
speaking about 4.2 inches. Keep
them in line like our names here.
Never center them.

MARTHA
Should I use (CONTINUED) and/or
(MORE) when a character's speech is
broken up by an action?

JOHN
No. Only use it when what a
character is saying is interrupted by a
page break.

(MORE)

JOHN (cont'd)
Like what just happened to me. It
shows that the speech began on the
preceding page.

> MARTHA
> What if the software I'm using
> automatically breaks the page on the
> slug line?

> JOHN
> Move it yourself to the next page.
> Never separate a slug line from the
> description it accompanies.

> MARTHA
> Gotcha. Now what if I want to do a
> flashback, maybe use narration?

> JOHN
> Just set it up and cut to it with a slug
> line. Clarify with a centered title if
> you like...

John pauses. And recalls a more innocent time a decade ago.

INT. JOHN'S BEDROOM – DAY

Wadded paper litters the floor, scene cards are tacked to a bulletin board, and a *Silence of the Lambs* poster is taped to the wall.

TEN YEARS EARLIER

Teenaged John types away on his brand new IBM Selectric.

> JOHN
> (voice-over)
> There was this strange contraption I used to use. What was it called? Oh, yes. A typewriter.

A distant telephone is heard ringing.

> MARTHA
> (voice-over)
> John...

INT. CLASSROOM – NIGHT

John snaps out of his reverie, the telephone still ringing.

> MARTHA
> Could be a good time to illustrate phone conversations.

Realizing the phone on the teacher's desk is ringing, John answers it.

> JOHN
> (into the phone)
> Hello?

INT. BOILER ROOM – NIGHT

Flies circle the head of the drooling phone SOLICITOR, beaded sweat mixing with nose drip on his upper lip.

SOLICITOR
(into the phone)
Hello, sir. Hope I'm not catching you
at a bad time.

INT. CLASSROOM – NIGHT

John's already annoyed, Martha curiously looking on.

JOHN
(into phone)
Well, I'm sort of in the middle of a
presentation.

SOLICITOR
(over phone)
I understand, sir...

INT. BOILER ROOM – NIGHT

SOLICITOR
(into phone)
This will only take a minute.

INT. CLASSROOM – NIGHT

JOHN
(into phone)
Not even.

Finding a whistle on the desk, he blows it into the phone.

> SOLICITOR
> (over phone)
> AHHHHHHH!!!!!!!!!!!!!

John smiles and hangs up, returning his attentions to Martha.

> MARTHA
> I noticed the parentheticals. Tell me about them.

> JOHN
> Put them on the line directly below the character's name, maybe .5 inch to the left. Use them sparingly to suggest a simple action or emotion. And be concise.

> MARTHA
> (excited)
> Like this!?

> JOHN
> Exactly. Anything more, write it as descriptive action.

John suddenly wraps her in his arms.

Caught by surprise, Martha tries pushing him away. Loving the feel of her body against his, he refuses to let go.

> MARTHA
> What the hell are you doing?

> JOHN
> Showing you an example.

> MARTHA
> (Washing up)
> Maybe you could show me a CUT TO so we can get out of this scene.

> JOHN
> I don't recommend using them. Just go to another slug line.

> MARTHA
> What about the occasional dissolve, to suggest a substantial transition of time and/or place?

> JOHN
> You mean, like this...?

DISSOLVE TO:

EXT. TROPICAL ISLAND – DAY

Palm trees sway in the warm breeze. Salt water laps gently at their feet.

Tan, rested, and ready to rock, John ogles Martha, standing before him in a skimpy bikini.

                    MARTHA
                  (perturbed)
            I can't believe you did that!

                    JOHN
            Come on, babe. Chill. You're the one
            who asked about dissolves.

                    MARTHA
            Anything else I should know? Other
            than the fact you're a jerk!

                    JOHN
            How about approaches to formatting
            beats in an action sequence?

                    MARTHA
            Allow me. First with mini slugs.

Martha glances down, seeing a

DEAD HALIBUT

Decaying at her feet. Snatching it off the sand, she slams John hard across the face with it.

> JOHN
>
Hey!

> MARTHA
> Then again, the same beats could be
> done straight-on. Like this.

Martha glances down, seeing a dead halibut decaying at her feet. Snatching if off the sand, she slams John hard across the face with it.

> JOHN
> Okay! Alright already.

Grimacing, he wipes a few rotten fish scales off his tongue.

> I get the picture.

> MARTHA
> Then get this.

She steps closer to him. Stares him in the eye.

> MARTHA
> Write your spec screenplay only in
> master scenes. That means no close
> ups, no angles, no mention of the
> camera's point of view whatsoever.
> That's

the job of the director and
cinematographer. Not the
writer.

                    JOHN
        And when it's finished?

                    MARTHA
        Photocopy it on three-hole paper,
        cover it with plain plastic card stock,
        and bind it with two 1-1/4 inch
        number 5 solid brass fasteners, one
        on top and one on the bottom.

He considers her words. And feels the impact of all
that's just happened.

                    JOHN
        You've changed, Martha.

                    MARTHA
        Some would say for the better.

She turns and walks away, leaving him picking another
rotten fish scale out of his mouth.

                    JOHN
            (grumbling to himself)
        I don't know. Think I preferred it
        when we were dodging bullets in the
        alley.

FADE OUT.

THE END

I recommend downloading the free screenwriting formatting program called CELTX. It will do all the tabs for you, and it remembers character names, scene headings, and various other things. CELTX does have a play-formatting program, but it is not the proper way to format plays, so I recommend not using it.

Television formatting follows the same principals as film formatting, except the action lines are in all CAPS, underneath each scene heading every character that is in the scene is listed in parenthesis, each scene is lettered, and after the teaser there are acts that change number after each commercial break.

	Plays	Films
Character Names above dialog	CAPS	CAPS
tab stop	3.0	3.0
Stage Directions	tab 3.5	
Scene Headings		1.0
Margins	1"	1"
Dialog margin	1"	Start at 2" stop at tab 4"
Parenthetical	3.5	2.5

Film Title Page

ELSON, THE FIRST CHRISTMAS ELF

by

Bob May

2010 © Bob May   100 United Way
All Rights Reserved   Anywhere, AR 7XXXX
                                 (501) XXX-XXXX
                                 bmay@uca.edu

Titles

"Would you pay $150.00 for a ticket to (insert the title of your script)?" The head of playwriting at UNLV (Jerry L. Crawford) asked this question when beginning his lecture on giving a title to a script. That is what a ticket for a Broadway show is selling for now.

Titles are very important. They attract an audience to a show, they can set the tone of the script, and they help tell an audience what the show is about.

There are two kinds of titles, literal and metaphorical. A literal title is just what it sounds like—a title that literally tells an audience what the show is about. *The Death and Life of Sneaky Fitch*, *The Actor's Nightmare*, or *The Dining Room* are examples of literal titles. *Cat on a Hot Tin Roof*, *Steel Magnolias*, or *A Flea in Her Ear* are examples of metaphorical titles.

Metaphorical titles are better because they garner interest in the show. One of my favorite metaphorical titles is *Good Will Hunting*. When I first heard it and hadn't seen the film, I thought it was about someone searching for goodwill. And I suppose it is to a degree. And a metaphorical title can have more than one meaning tied to theme. After seeing the film, I realized the title meant, good, Will Hunting. Will Hunting being the protagonist's name.

Exercise: Titles

Create a list of titles for a new play.

Now change those same titles to metaphorical titles.

CHAPTER 9

Some Other Pointers

The following tips have been learned, taught, and practiced over the years. I am constantly learning new things from teaching, reading others' scripts, and writing my own.

Just Write – Fix It Later

Trust yourself and your rough scenario. Write a first draft and then go back and fix it. In the book, *Bird By Bird* by Anne Lamott, she has some very good advice in a chapter called "Shitty First Drafts." She writes, "The only way I can get anything written at all is to write really, really, really shitty first drafts. The first draft is the child's draft, where you let it all pour out and then let it romp all over the place, knowing that no one is going to see it and that you can shape it later. You just let this childlike part of you channel whatever voices and visions come through and onto the page."

Lamott continues, "Almost all good writing begins with terrible first efforts. You need to start somewhere.

Start by getting something–anything–down on paper. A friend of mine says that the first draft is the down draft–you just get it down. The second draft is the up draft–you fix it up. You try to say what you have to say more accurately. And the third draft is the dental draft, where you check every tooth, to see if it's loose or cramped or decayed, or even, God help us, healthy."[5]

Stephen Sondheim says, "The worst thing you can do is censor yourself as the pencil hits the paper. You must not edit until you get it all on paper. If you can put everything down, stream-of-consciousness, you'll do yourself a service."[6]

I even do this with letters I write. No one ever reads the original draft. It is all about the rewrites.

Rewrites

Why is "Rewrites" separate from the above tip? "Just Write–Fix it Later" is all about the first draft. "Rewrites" is about all the drafts to follow.

In Neil Simon's autobiography *Rewrites*, he says he rewrote his first play, *Come Blow Your Horn*, twenty-two times before he was satisfied with it and it finally was produced.

If you have not read his two autobiographies, put them on your reading list. They are a website worth of great playwriting knowledge.

Writing is rewriting and rewriting. Learn form the following tips and keep rewriting.

---

5 Lamont, Anne. *Bird by Bird, Some Instructions on Writing and Life*, Anchor Books, a division of Random House, Inc., NY, pgs. 21-27.
6 Sondheim, Stephen. BrainyQuotes.com. June 2015.

Have a Reading

It doesn't matter how many times you read your script on the computer screen, silently or aloud. The next step is to have a reading. Remember, dialogue is meant to be heard, not read.

Organize the reading yourself if it's not being done in a class. It is very helpful in understanding your script by hearing it read aloud by actors. Do not be one of the actors. You need to sit back and listen to your words. Finding good actors to read your words is also a must. Actors do all that psychoanalysis of characters and think up things that never entered your mind as you were writing. That's cool. Learn from it. Take the good and the bad and soar with your discoveries.

Neil Simon says, "Hearing dialogue on the stage or screen is completely different than reading it silently from the printed page. In one, you hear what the actor says; in the other, you hear in your head what you imagined the character sounds like. Oftentimes audiences are disappointed with the film version of a book they read. The actor now playing the role doesn't sound like the character they heard in their heads."[7]

Learn from the reading, and rewrite.

Production is the Ultimate

There is nothing better than having your play produced. The rehearsal period is much better than

---

7 Simon, Neil. *Rewrites: A Memoir.* New York, Simon & Schuster, 1996.

just a reading because there is more time to discover and see what works or needs work.

You are not alone. The actors are working beat-by-beat and unit-by-unit through the script and their parts, discovering objectives. Directors have broken the play into units and have a vision. All this input really helps you see the pros and cons. There is time to fix things using the actors.

Then the ultimate test is seeing how things play in front of a real, live audience. All the writing, directing, and acting only makes sense when you can see and hear the reaction of a live audience.

I Hate To Write But Love To Have Written

I think I am paraphrasing a statement about jogging. "I hate to run, but I love to have ran." The endorphins kick in and oh what a great feeling. If you are serious about writing, you must set aside a time that you do just that and do it everyday. Neil Simon did not write at home. He rented an office and went to it every day, just like a job, from eight to five, and wrote. He sat in his office and wrote. That doesn't mean each day was a successful one, but he was there to find out.

I've never had to do that. I've been successful writing at home. I do have a room that is designated as my office and when I go into it, I am there to work. I have been on a routine of writing from seven p.m. to one a.m. every night for the past twenty-two years. It's not easy. And it can create problems in any relationship.

You must find a time that you set aside and write everyday and the place where you do it. Make it your space and only use it to write.

No, Playwriting is Not More Important Than a Relationship

Several of my relationships suffered because the writing was more important than they were. I've tried to not let the obsession with writing do the same thing in my current relationship. Luckily, I have an understanding spouse. Just make sure to spend some time with the other half who inspires you to write.

Writing a Play is Not Really Real Life

Writing a play is a reflection of life. It is not real life. Putting real life on the stage was tried in the late nineteenth and early twentieth century. It was called naturalism, and much of the writing didn't work because there wasn't any dramaturgical shaping. There needs to be structure in drama. There needs to be PASTO, something at stake, an MDQ.

Even a script based on a true story is not real. The events are real, but they probably didn't happen in a two-hour time period, and if it is a network TV movie, it didn't happen with climactic moments every eight minutes, right before a commercial.

Think about a real life situation and then think about what the important events in that situation were. Learning to separate the important events in real life situations is a lesson well learned in playwriting.

Let's take the first fifteen minutes of a class. If I were going to dramatize those fifteen minutes, I wouldn't put all fifteen minutes into a script. I might establish where we were by showing a student or two entering the classroom (the protagonist would be one of those students), then the teacher enters (establish some of what teacher does to begin class), set an MDQ (let's say there is going to be a vote on which student script is going to be produced by the class), portions of the readings of the scripts, or parts of the pitches the writers give the class, and set up a competition (an antagonist). Depending on the length of the script, all those events could be done in thirty to sixty seconds. So fifteen minutes of real time has been reduced to 1/15 of real time.

Understanding structure is the key. Well, one of the keys.

Repeating Information That the Audience Already Knows

In *True Blood*, Bill ends up missing at the end of season two. Sookie's brother asks her what's wrong? She looks at him with sad eyes and then embraces him. She doesn't have to tell him. Or the audience didn't need to hear her tell him because they already know this information.

When writing a script, remember that you are writing it for the audience. If they already know information another character doesn't know, there is no reason to repeat that information. There are ways to get around repeating the known information. If you do repeat it, what new information can be revealed to the audience by repeating it?

Davey's Thirteen Commandments

Davey Marlin-Jones was my mentor and friend while I was in the MFA Playwriting Program at UNLV. I really think Davey was Dionysus reincarnated. The second coming of the God of Theatre had come, and I was lucky enough to be blessed by his teachings. Davey is theatre.

Davey said these are not THE Thirteen commandments—there are probably 134. Here are thirteen the playwright might embrace. You probably can write a great play and ignore them, but the writing will take a lot longer.

1. A dramatic event is one that MUST make something else happen. (See David Ball, *Backwards and Forwards*, Chapter 1).

2. When you write character descriptions to aid yourself in the building of your play, remember no playwright paints still life. Verbs and purpose must be implicit within your character descriptions.

3. If there is no disparity between what your characters are saying and what they actually are doing, you probably don't write theatre.

4. Remember when you write a set description, you are creating an environment. That environment is the bow; your characters are the arrows. The environment

must catapult your characters into their respective actions.

5. Conflict often exists without direct confrontation. Sometimes conflict intensifies by what is NOT said in response: "Lend me five bucks." "Nice tie."

6. Good playwrights write for actors. Playwrights learn what actors do. Read Boleslavsky, *Acting: The First Six Lessons.* Actors are not feelers. They are doers. In playing a specific purpose, only then is the emotion the residual. Write accordingly.

7. As a playwright, keep stage directions to a minimum. Worry about what happens, not HOW it happens. That's why directors earn salaries.

8. All characters you write must be empathetic. Each person you create must be able to entice a first-rate actor to play the role. If you don't care about your characters, how can you expect your cast and audience to empathize?

9. Understand each character's ear. Characters in plays do not read each other's lines. They *hear* each other, *mis-hear* each other and *refuse to hear* each other. That's very different from simply coming in on cue.

10. The playwright is an orchestrator of her individual character's energies. Those energies spring from the separate characters' "clocks" and needs.

11. Dramatic tension is never a constant. As a character's objective is pursued and the culmination of that pursuit is thwarted, tension is earned and then builds.

12. As your play builds, raise the stakes by intensifying the character verbs.

13. A play is comprised of increments of action: not unlike a series of prize-fighting rounds where characters win, lose or fight to a draw. Each round is a dramatic beat. These beats compromise the vertebrae in the spines of your characters, and the sum of those vertebrae comprise the spine of the play and the addressing of the play's Major Dramatic Question.

Culled from the wisdom of Jerry L. Crawford, Richard Boleslavsky, David Ball, William Ball, and the ages.

Read a Play a Day

Read a play a day was the advice I got from my undergraduate mentor, Dick Cermele, and my first reaction was probably the same as yours is now. I don't have time to read a play a day. But, I found that I did and the most important lesson I learned from that was that all plays are structurally the same. The plots may be as different as night and day, but all successfully written plays share the same common element — structure.

The more you read, the more these Pointers will come into focus.

EXERCISE: Reading of the Script

Organize a reading of a script that you like and listen to the difference between your reading all the parts in the script silently and your reading all the parts aloud.

CONCLUSION

These pointers are the culmination of fifty years of reading scripts, reading about writing scripts, talking to others who write scripts, taking classes about writing scripts, teaching classes on writing scripts, and writing hundreds of scripts.

Now take what you've learned from reading these pointers and combine them with your own pointers, then apply them in your scriptwriting. And write. Write every day, preferably at the same time, for the same amount of time. Find a space that is your writing space. Treat writing as a job.

The more you write, the better you will get. And the better you get, the more you will write.

About the Author

Bob May began his theater career as an actor in 1967 with a small role in *Kiss Me Kate* at Ft. Lauderdale High School (FL). Acting took a backseat to directing while he earned a BA in Theater from St. Cloud State University (MN) in 1972. Since that time he has directed over four hundred and fifty productions at various educational, community, and professional theaters across the country, winning numerous awards for his directing.

While directing, he was also writing plays. In 1994 Bob earned an MFA in Playwriting from The University of Nevada, Las Vegas, and directing took a backseat to writing. To date, over fifty of his plays have been produced, with productions around the world, and twenty-two have been published. The most popular are *Beanie and the Bamboozling Book Machine, Elson-The First Christmas Elf,* and *Jack and Bella: From Beanstalk to Broadway.*

He was the Artistic Director and in-house playwright for the Conway, Arkansas-based Children's Theatre to Go from 2002-2008. They produced his work exclusively, including *Crystal and the Christmas Snowman; A Different Kind of Nutcracker;* and *Elson, the First Christmas Elf* (all published in the collection: *Snowmen, Elves, and Nutcrackers* by Baker's Plays); *Jack and Bella: From Beanstalk to Broadway-a musical* (published by Heuer Publishing); *Cinderella and the Fairy Godfather, Alice in Wonderland, Snow White and the Magic Mirror,* and *Hocus Pocus Horticulture* (all published by Playscripts, Inc.) and *The Great Santa Claus Reindeer Roundup* (published by Brooklyn Publishing).

In 2008 he wrote The Gulf Coastal Plains Region episode for the Arkansas Educational Television Network (PBS) program *The Great Experience of Arkansas: An Amazing Journey Through Six Regions.* He also produced, directed, and wrote the documentary on ghost hunting titled *The Ladies of the Night* in 2011. And his book *Postcard Pointers to the Performer* is published by Dominion Publications, Cedar Rapids, Iowa. *The Process of Directing: From Concept to Curtain* is published by Skye Bridge Publishing.

Mr. May began teaching in higher education in 1983 and currently teaches Playwriting and Screenwriting at the University of Central Arkansas. Since moving to Arkansas, he has written four sequels to his popular play *Beanie and the Bamboozling Book Machine;* they are *Beanie and the Bamboozling Horror Machine, Beanie* and the *Bamboozling Adventure Machine* (all published by Samuel French, Inc.), *Gidget's Gadget to Bamboozle Beanie* (published by Playscripts Inc.), and *The Wizard of Bamboozlement.*

He and his wife, Cathy, have a blended family of five children and five grandchildren. Mr. May is a member of The Dramatists Guild of America.

PUBLISHED WORKS

BOOKS

Postcard Pointers to the Performer. Published by Dominion Publications, Cedar Rapids, IA

Scriptwriting Structure: To-the-Point Pointers. Published by Skye Bridge Publishing, Asheville. NC

The Process of Play Directing: From Concept to Curtain. Published by Skye Bridge Publishing, Asheville, NC

PLAYS

Beanie and the Bamboozling Book Machine - a fantasy-adventure – published by Samuel French, Inc., New York, NY

Beanie and the Bamboozling Horror Machine - a sequel - published by Samuel French, Inc.

Beanie and the Bamboozling Adventure Machine - a second sequel –published by Samuel French, Inc.

The Andrew is Dead Story - a play in one act - published by I. E. Clark, Inc., Schelenburg, TX

9th Inning Wedding - a play in one act - published by I. E. Clark, Inc.

9th Inning Wedding – also published in the textbook, *The Golden Stage: Dramatic Activities for Older Adults* by Ann McDonough, Ph.D. Kendall/Hunt, publisher.

Broadway Memories - a musical revue – published in *The Golden Stage*

Concerned Citizens - a short play - published in the collection Short Stuff: 10- to 20- Minute Plays for Mature Actors, Dramatic Publishing,   Chicago, IL

Cinderella and the Fairy Godfather - published by Playscripts, Inc., New York, NY

Alice and Wonderland - published by Playscripts, Inc.

Snow White and the Magic Mirror - published by Playscripts, Inc.

Gidget's Gadget to Bamboozle Beanie - published by Playscripts, Inc.

Snowmen, Elves, and Nutcrackers: Three Christmas Plays
Crystal and the Christmas Snowman
Elson, The First Christmas Elf
A Different Kind of Nutcracker published by Baker's Plays, New York, NY

Hocus Pocus Horticulture - published by Playscripts, Inc., New York, NY

Go To ... a ten-minute absurdist play, published in Exquisite Corpse Literary Journal, Jan 2009, and also published by Heuer Publishing, Cedar Rapids, IA

Jack and Bella: From Beanstalk to Broadway – a musical – published by Heuer Publishing, Cedar Rapids, IA

The Great Santa Claus Reindeer Roundup – published by Brooklyn Publishers, Cedar Rapids, IA

Lightning Source UK Ltd.
Milton Keynes UK
UKOW05f0307151216
289984UK00016B/392/P